This edition published in 2013
by Notting Hill Editions Ltd
Newcombe House, 45 Notting Hill Gate
London W11 3LQ

Designed by FLOK Design, Berlin, Germany
Typeset by CB editions, London

Printed and bound
by Memminger MedienCentrum, Memmingen, Germany

A CIP record for this book is available from the British Library

ISBN 978-1-907-90358-8

www.nottinghilleditions.com

Francis Bacon was one of the iconic figures of modern art, a painter who transformed the way we see and experience the human body. Mirroring Bacon's famous triptychs, Jonathan Littell's three essays engage with the artist's contorted figures and portraits, his screaming popes and apes, his flanks of beef and his umbrellas. In 'A Day at the Prado', Littell analyses Bacon's painting in the light of Velazquez and Goya – two artists who deeply influenced him. In 'The Grammar of Francis Bacon', the artist's portraits of his lover George Dyer before and after his suicide in 1971 provide a key to the hidden correspondences between the figures he painted. Littell then, in 'The True Image', looks at the history of icon painting and photography before returning to Bacon, questioning the very meaning of truth in art. Erudite and deeply personal, Jonathan Littell's exegesis on the work of a major twentieth-century artist seeks to lay bare the sinews of Francis Bacon's tormented art.

Praise for *The Kindly Ones*:

'An extraordinarily powerful novel that leads the stunned reader on a journey through some of the darkest recesses of European history . . . reveals something that is desperate and depressing but profoundly important, now as ever.' – *Observer*

'The book rises magnificently to its own occasions, building out of its fact crammed but stately sentences a vast and phosphorescent tableaux vivants seething with Dantesque detail.'
– *Guardian*

Jonathan Littell was born in New York of American parents, and grew up mainly in France. His novel *Les Bienveillantes* won the Prix Goncourt in 2006, as well as the Académie Française's Prix de Littérature. Jonathan Littell usually writes in French. *Triptych* was written in English, and this is its first English-language publication.

Jonathan Littell

–

TRIPTYCH

–

Three Studies after Francis Bacon

. . . Just as if illogicality were a comfort, as if thought were allowed laughter, as if error were the road, love the acceptable world and chance a proof of eternity.

– Hans Bellmer,
Little Anatomy of the Physical Unconscious

Notting Hill Editions

Contents

– A Day at the Prado –

S ome time ago I was at the Prado looking at paintings by Francis Bacon. The Prado is truly a marvellous museum, probably, thanks to the wildly eclectic and aristocratically sensuous taste of the so-called Catholic Kings and their successors, one of the finest in the world. Francis Bacon also liked the Prado a great deal. He went there often, from the late 1940s onward, alone or with friends or lovers. The last few years of his life, when he came to Madrid, he called up Manuela Mena Marqués, the Prado curator in charge of the eighteenth century and of Goya, and asked her to take him around on a Monday, when the museum is closed and no one but the painter and his chaperone intruded on the quiet of its vast rooms and halls, filled with pictures. And then one day, long after Bacon's death, the director of the Prado asked Manuela Mena to curate a retrospective of the British artist's work, right here in the same museum he enjoyed so much. Manuela Mena, it turns out, is a very kind person, and also someone who very much likes talking about painting, and not just with painters. This is as good a reason as any other to go to the Prado. There is a lot to be learned by looking at pictures together with someone

3

who not only knew the painter but knows how to look at paintings, how to read painting.

When you enter the gallery, in the new wing of the Prado, the first thing facing you is, of course, the small searing orange panels of the *Three Studies for Figures at the Base of a Crucifixion*. Bacon always claimed this 1944 triptych as his 'inaugural' painting, affirming, rather exaggeratedly, that he had destroyed everything he had produced before (in fact, his delicate 1933 *Crucifixion* hangs right next to the *Three Studies*; as for the long-necked toothy eyeless biomorphs of this 'first' triptych, they already appear in a 1943 *Figure Getting Out of a Car* and an untitled 1944 painting). Manuela Mena loves this triptych. 'Here, we have three different presentations of the figures. The one on the right is directly in the light, in full command. The one in the center is beginning to doubt; the one on the left shows fear, submission. And the one in the center is like that because of the other two, which are both facing and threatening it. The right figure appears as male; its leg is solidly planted on the ground, in a patch of grass [Bacon's father, a retired army captain, trained racehorses]; the left figure is a semblance of a mother.' While the source image of the head of the left-panel biomorph has been unequivocally identified as a photograph of the medium Eva Carrière published in 1920 by Baron von Schrenck-Notzing, Bacon's appropriation of this image may not have been as random as he certainly would have claimed: on the wall opposite the triptych, as chance would have it, hangs a photograph of the future painter, age four, lovingly gazing up at his mother; the curves of her face, her chin, her hair, strongly echo those shown in profile by Eva Carrière, as painted by her son over three decades later. And the middle figure? 'It combines male and female, as Bacon so often does when he represents himself.' The back of the figure indeed resembles the glans of a penis; but it also mirrors, in shape and colour, the buttocks of Velázquez's so-called *Rokeby Venus*, the *Toilet of Venus* that Bacon must have seen as early as the 1930s in the London National Gallery, and which had an over-whelming influence on him. 'If you don't understand the *Rokeby Venus* you don't understand my painting,' he once declared to Hugh Davies, a young American art historian. In the article she wrote for the catalog, Manuela Mena discusses this image and its migration: 'Velázquez [for the *Venus*] was inspired by the reclin-ing figure . . . of the classical *Hermaphrodite* sculpture [a marble copy of which he brought back from Italy, to make the bronze casting now in the Prado, right in front of *Las Meninas*], which he turned into a woman, and which Bacon, as a proof of the metamorphosis of images carried out by all artists, then reconverted into a man.' Back to the *Three Studies*: while the right-panel 'male' figure barks aggressively, and the left-panel 'fe-male' figure resentfully cocks its long neck, both pas-sive and menacing, the center figure, its eyes covered in dropping white bandages – and if we indeed accept this figure as a metaphorical self-portrait, it is astonishing to note that the sole photograph of Bacon's dead body, taken in the morgue of the Ruber Clinic in Madrid by a shameless paparazzo, shows him with his eyes and forehead covered with a similar large white band, bearing his name – hisses or screeches in fear at its predicament. Both of us contemplate this image for long minutes in silence before Manuela Mena concludes, sadly: 'He never had any way out, as a child.'

—

When Francis Bacon came to the Prado with Manuela Mena, he wanted to see only two painters, Velázquez and Goya. Nothing else, not Bosch and not Brueghel, not Titian or Rubens, nothing. Even the bronze hermaphrodite in front of *Las Meninas* wasn't worth a glance to him: 'Hockney likes it a lot,' mentions Manuela Mena, 'but Bacon hardly even looked at it.' He would go up very close to the paintings and gaze at them for a long time, without a word. He knew them by heart, of course; but he would always find something new in them, a solution to a particular problem he was facing just then. Over the years he had learned and taken a lot from all the pictures he looked at, far more than just figures, such as the Roman soldier falling backward in El Greco's great *Resurrection*, which reappears in the upside-down nudes he repeated throughout the late 1950s and 1960s, or, famously, the sour and dominating Velázquez *Pope Innocent X* he painted well over forty or fifty times, unsuccessfully in his own mind, but compulsively. Like all painters, Bacon was first and foremost concerned with the way paint is applied. 'Look at the black line between sleeve and flesh,' points out Manuela Mena in front of the 1945 *Figure in a Landscape*. 'It's the same as in the *Meninas*. And here, in this *Pope* [the 1951 *Pope I*], the glossy black right behind the head: all classical painters do that, to pull the head off the flat background.' Bacon's use of a broad line of bright colour to outline a body already has its precedent in several of Goya's Black Paintings, especially the *Saturn* where Goya uses a vivid red not only to outline the white remains of the figure being devoured but the greedy clutching fingers of Saturn as well. And Bacon clearly had the neck of the *Rokeby Venus* in his mind's eye when he painted, over and over again, the necks and backs of nude males, especially of his lover George Dyer (look for instance at the 1970 *Three Studies of the Male Back*); nor did he ever forget the picture's strikingly modern palette, a bold combination of crimson, white, metallic gray and pale luminous flesh, which keeps recurring in his work, as so many of his paintings, from the 1949 *Head II* to the 1988 *Second Version of Triptych 1944*, can attest. What was the most important thing he learned from Velázquez, I ask Manuela Mena? She thinks for a few instants before answering: 'His essentiality, reducing the brushstrokes to the minimum. Velázquez puts on one brushstroke and that's enough. It's the purest economy of means.

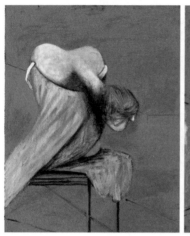

III, IV

And also the sense of space. The sense of space is absolutely Velázquez. Again, look at the *Venus*.' To paint with a Velázquezian sense of economy has profound implications for the painter's attitude: no matter what Bacon may have claimed ('intelligence has never made art, has never made painting') it requires a powerful pictorial intelligence. 'Velázquez painted very quickly, but he thought for a long time before laying a brush on the canvas. So when he began, he had a very clear idea of what he was going to do. A writer can take out words, but a painter can't really remove paint. And so the only way for him to paint economically is to think in advance of what he is going to do.'

In 1971, in an interview with Marguerite Duras, Bacon says of Goya: 'He has wedded his forms with air. It seems that his paintings are made with the matter of air.' He meant something very specific by this, which Manuela Mena shows me in front of Goya's great *Tres de Mayo*, upstairs in the older part of the empty museum. Goya first primed his giant canvas with an even reddish beige coating; and when he figures flesh, in this painting and its companion *Dos de Mayo*, the hands of the corpses lying on the ground, the faces of the men about to die, or of the French soldiers about to fire at them, there is in actuality no paint there, just a few brushstrokes for the outline, a single brushstroke for an eyebrow or an eye, at most a quick light greenish-brown wash: Goya is painting here with literally *nothing*. In places, like the wall above the condemned men

or the leather shoulder straps of the French soldiers, he actually scraped paint away to reach the effect he wanted. You have to climb on a chair to see it – or start roaming on your computer over the surface of the high-definition image the Prado has produced in collaboration with Google Earth – but it's there whether you notice it or not, it's how this extraordinary painting is made. And though Bacon would have seen only very few Goyas until the 1950s at the earliest, he somehow already had learned this lesson, which he began to apply with such marvellous delicacy to paint the left arm and buttocks of his 1949 *Study from the Human Body*, only taking it a step further than Goya, by leaving the canvas raw, unprimed, simply dragging the dry pigments over it in a few rapid strokes. 'It's amazing how he could have done that without Goya,' comments Manuela Mena in front of this haunting figure, stepping through a sort of thin gauzy curtain into the darkness, its head bent in patient resignation. 'Goya of course could never have left the canvas unprimed, that never would have occurred to him. But the technique is the same,' the 'technical imagination' as Bacon named it. Bacon also took a great deal from Degas, from Picasso, of course, even from his contemporaries. For all his contemptuous dismissal of Rothko ('the most dreary paintings that have ever been made' is how he put it in a 1985 interview) he grappled closely with some of the same pictorial problems as the great abstract expressionist. Bacon's borrowings from Rothko's 'mature style' can be traced back to his 1959 stay at the artist's colony in St Ives, where he painted a number of 'reclining figures': whereas these reversed figures can be seen as citations of El Greco or, as Martin Harrison proposes in his book *In Camera*, of Rodin's *Iris* and *Flying Figure*, several of them are set on an abstracted background of horizontal panes of colour, strongly reminiscent of Rothko's preparatory sketches, or even in some cases (the 1959 *Lying Figure*, for instance) of one of his major canvases. There are obviously fundamental differences in treatment: in Rothko, the rectangular forms never reach the edge of the canvas, they hover in front of the ground, whereas when Bacon treats his backgrounds in a Rothkoian manner, they remain backgrounds. But many of the formal problems adressed are comparable, the question of the tonal relations of the colours (as opposed to their values), the tension between the flattening of the picture space and the illusion of depth, the relation of the size of the picture to the size of the viewer. Bacon obviously looked long and hard at Rothko, and years after his death continued working both with and against him: consider, for instance, the crimson background in the outer panels of the 1988 *Second Version of Triptych 1944*. His *Blood on Pavement*, also probably painted in 1988, one of the last paintings of his life, *is* a late Rothko; take away the stain of blood and that's what's left, a black, white, greenish-gray Rothko, with its terribly free treatment of the paint, its drips, its unfinished edges,

VII

and the narrow pale gray line between the bottom two panes of paint: had Bacon been more honest, or less of a prankster, he would have called this picture *Study After Rothko* (here, again, Bacon's planes run to the edge of the picture; but there is a Rothko precedent for that, a similarly black and gray 1969 untitled painting, now in the collection of Christopher Rothko). *Blood* is such a transparent citation that one feels that Bacon has only added the blood itself – the sole figurative element, treated very much in the manner of Goya's lacquered bloodstains in the *Tres de Mayo* – as a joke, in order to say to us, 'Look, you see I can do a Rothko, just look at it, the only difference between this and a Rothko is the bloodstain, which I put there because you expect it from me, so that the painting will tell you, "I could be a Rothko, but as you can see I'm a Bacon."' Of course Francis Bacon's pictorial language is, in many ways, antithetical to the languages of abstract expressionism; yet often both seem to be coming at the same thing from opposite sides. Which is not something that could be said of his relationship to his great predecessors: it may have been entirely anachronistic (as Manuela Mena puts it, 'For him, seventeenth century, eighteenth century, nineteenth century, it's all the same'), but he was not pursuing the same objectives as they; the stakes had dramatically altered, and ever since the appearance of photography, the painter could no longer be satisfied with what Bacon dismissed as 'illustration', another term perhaps for what

Foucault designates in his landmark study of *Las Meninas* as 'classical representation'. 'Although I may use, or appear to use, traditional methods,' Bacon told the British art critic David Sylvester in the early 1970s, 'I want those methods to work for me in a very different way to that in which they have worked before or for which they were originally formed . . . although I may use what's called the techniques that have been handed down, I'm trying to make out of them something that is radically different to what those techniques have made before.' Or, as he put it rather crudely as early as 1949 in a *Time* magazine interview: 'One of the problems is to paint like Velázquez but with the texture of a hippopotamus skin.' Bacon would not use the hippo skin texture for long; it was just one of his tricks on the way, one of the devices he tried out to nail down the thing he was after all along: the violence of reality, incarnated in paint. The violence of paint.

—

For the German art historian Hans Belting, 'The experience of death has been one of the most powerful engines of the human production of images.' This was certainly the case for Bacon, who probably knew even before he began to paint that a corpse, as Blanchot put it, is already an image. And this is why, for Bacon in his practice as for Belting in his theory, the medium, which figures through its presence the absence of that which is represented (just like the corpse figures the absence of the dead person), is so important. 'That which is matter in the world of bodies and things is medium in the world of images,' writes Belting. In this medium – and not just any medium, but the royal medium of Western painting, oil paint, 'such a fluid and curious medium' in his own words – Francis Bacon would spend his entire life painting bodies, trying to seize the most secret sensations of human bodies, trying to obtain a precise representation of how inhabiting that specific body felt, on a given day. And often, through the grace of his technical imagination and his surrender to chance, through his infinite tenderness and his pitiless love in the gaze and in the application of paint, he succeeded: and what we see on a Bacon canvas is not how a body *looks*, something he had little interest in, but how a body *feels*, feels in its skin and bones and sinews as it is doing whatever it is that it is doing at that particular moment, walking, standing, smoking, shitting, fucking, lying in anguish on a mattress, sitting in great despair in a chair, dying. This would make of him the finest painter of flesh since Rembrandt (and perhaps Rubens, but I don't really like Rubens; and neither did Bacon, for that matter). His critics and viewers generally saw his figures as creatures distorted, warped, tortured ('Very often the people you paint are beautiful,' asserts the French critic Franck Maubert to Bacon in a 1987 TV interview, 'and once they are painted they are ugly') not realizing that his furious deformations were precisely what was needed to turn beautiful people into beautiful paintings. Those he painted saw it immediately: 'They are exactly like me, my personality,' averred Henrietta Moraes, one of Bacon's main models in the 1960s, to interviewers who clearly didn't comprehend what she was talking about. 'There's an eyebrow that's suddenly exactly like me, or a bit of an eye. I know it's me.' Bacon himself often said that he didn't paint flesh, that he painted meat; maybe though this was another one of his little private jokes (which I probably would never have gotten if my nine-year-old son, catching sight of the Prado catalog, hadn't cried out in horror: 'Poor man! To be called *lard*, that's terrible'). He also always insisted that he didn't know where his images came from. 'They just fall in like slides,' he claimed, they appeared in his head like the images of dreams, which make of the body, as in the classical dualistic conception, 'a theatre of images of unknown origin' (Belting, again). Of course, Bacon didn't need to know more, on the contrary, like all painters he thought with his paintbrushes; as the seventeenth-century Spanish-Italian painter and theoretician Vicente Carducho put it: 'The brush commands the mind.' Yet as with all images, his are charged with meaning, meaning that is there for us to read. The art historian John Moffitt, writing about Velázquez, talks about 'the often cryptic, emotionally charged, and highly learned symbolic language which underlies so much of the imagery of this period – profound truths veiled in mere reality, as it were.' His words could just as well apply to Bacon, who may have taken more even from Velázquez than his pope, his Venus and his sense of economy. Bacon, when he came to the Prado, looked a great deal at Velázquez's supreme masterwork, *Las Meninas* (which Moffitt, echoing what Manuela Mena argues about the importance of pictorial intelligence, cites as evidence of 'the mental process of *disegno interno* which necessarily precedes the physical act of *disegno esterno*'). Manuela Mena, who looked at it with him, happens to be the author of the latest major reinterpretation of this painting, still controversial though in my view irresistible in its cold, seductive logic. After the last restoration of the canvas, in 1986, she began looking once again at the X-rays first made in 1965. These X-rays, as every scholar knew, show a different figure under the self-portrait of the artist, to the left of the painting; some believed it was Velázquez himself in a different position, others thought it might be another person, but no one knew why he was there, or the reason for the change. Slowly, taking into account new elements that had appeared in the restoration, Manuela Mena began to understand that Velázquez had originally painted, below a draped curtain that is now also gone, a young man, a page wearing an Italian costume (with its collar flopping down rather than rising around the neck), who was presenting to the infanta Margarita Teresa a stick-like object which was probably the royal baton, the emblem of the king's command over the army. 'Now this is of course impossible,' she says,

'a woman could never touch the baton of command.'
Yet the baton is there, you can even divine its outline
with the naked eye, under the overpainting, rising
diagonally behind the head of the kneeling maid of
honor, Doña María Augustina Sarmiento, toward the
mirror showing the image of the king and the queen;
and as cleverly as Velázquez later tried to mask them,
you can still make out, even in a good reproduction,
just above the infanta's right sleeve, the fingers of the
little girl reaching up and back to accept the baton. For
that, according to Manuela Mena, was indeed the initial objective of the painting: to help render acceptable
the unacceptable. In 1656, when this first version was
painted, Philip IV's sole male child, Baltasar Carlos,
had been dead for ten years, and, in the fraught context
of the war with France and his endless dithering over
the wedding of his eldest daughter, María Teresa, he
had finally decided to make the five-year-old princess
his heir, a politically difficult and risky choice, which
would inevitably meet with strong resistance from the
usually obedient Cortes and the powerful landed aris-
tocracy that furnished most of its members. 'And so,'
says Mena, 'he told Velázquez: I need a painting that
will make it acceptable, that will show all those people that they should accept my decision and that there
is no problem. And Velázquez thought long and hard
about it before he began painting. And this is what he
created. Everything in this painting was put there to
say one thing and one thing only: this little girl, whom

VIII

everyone knew to be an undisciplined madcap, will be the next queen of Spain, and it will all be fine, just fine.' A dynastic painting, then, in which the power of the king radiates from the mirror – the crucial specular symbol of this power – to bathe the whole room, while his daughter, her little body carefully poised in a studied attitude of self-possession, accepts the emblems of command, before an assembly that looks on quietly, calmly, happily; even the dog is so undisturbed by this momentous event that it sleeps, and the dwarf Nicolasito Pertusato nudges it playfully with his foot, trying to get it to look too.

Then, in 1657, another son was born to the king, Felipe Prospero, who was immediately proclaimed Prince of Asturias and heir to the throne, and this made the great painting suddenly obsolete – worse yet, dangerous. But Velázquez, who knew he had painted here one of the masterpieces of his age, could not accept having it destroyed. 'Let me change it,' he must have asked the king. 'I can change it, and you will still have a great painting.' The picture probably remained in his studio, perhaps even turned to the wall, until finally he found his solution. And this solution is what we see now: gone is the page with the baton; in his place stands the painter, proudly bearing on his chest the *Cruz Roja del Orden de Santiago* he received only in 1659, his brush poised above his palette, about to be applied to a canvas hidden from our view, its back turned to us (just as, one might imagine, it may have been turned to him for those two long years in the studio), about to paint the painting we are looking at, this wonderful courtly fiction now called *El Cuadro de la Familia de Felipe IV* and later known as *Las Meninas*, or rather about to paint the painter into the painting, to transform the obsolete dynastic painting into a splendid little game, based, as the French art historian Daniel Arasse puts it, on a simple story: One day, as the painter was painting the king and queen in the gallery of the Cuarto Bajo del Príncipe, the turbulent little infanta, impatient for her parents, broke into the room with her retinue and watched him work. A courtly fiction, yes, but one still imbued through and through with the full power of the dynastic original, the power of the king that Velázquez, with all his painterly intelligence, his technical imagination, had painted into the original, and which nothing could now remove, even as the story changed. In the library of the king, in the Alcázar, figured a volume Velázquez had certainly read, Vicente Carducho's 1633 *Dialogos de la Pintura*; and on the last page, which John Moffitt evokes in his discussion of *Las Meninas*, appears an engraving that stands as an emblem of painting: a paintbrush just touching a bare white canvas, leaving no mark but only a shadow; above, worked into a laurel wreath, an enigmatic Latin phrase, POTENTIA AD ACTUM TAMQUAM TABULA RASA ('Power/Potentiality is to the Act/Determination like a tabula rasa'); and below it, four lines of verse:

En la que tabla rasa tanto excede,
que vee todas las cosas en potencia,
solo el pínçel con soberana ciençia,
reducir la potencia al acto puede.

On the tabla rasa which is so excellent,
that it has the power to see all things,
only the paintbrush with its sovereign science,
can turn power into an act.

This is what Velázquez's paintbrush is about to do in *Las Meninas*: to resolve an infinite but unrealized power into a single act, an act of painting. Francis Bacon, who thought Velázquez 'an amazingly mysterious painter', never represented himself with a paintbrush in hand (the closest he ever came is a 1966 *Study for a Portrait*, in which the figure mimicks Velázquez's pose in *Las Meninas*, palette in hand, yet without the brush itself). But when he wanted to paint himself into a painting as a painter, he still turned to *Las Meninas*, taking from it not the painter and his poised brush, but the canvas with its back turned to the viewer, the edge of its frame glowing with light. Manuela Mena, in her essay on 'Bacon and Spanish Painting', convincingly argues that the naked child in the 1961 *Paralytic Child Walking on All Fours (from Muybridge)*, advancing 'with a movement neither entirely human nor entirely animal' toward the beautifully depicted empty stretcher of a canvas, which of course it can never stand up to reach, 'becomes almost a self-portrait of the artist.'

The same stretcher, she also notes, reappears with its canvas mounted in the central panel of the 1971 *Triptych – In Memory of George Dyer*: the last thing Dyer sees in the stairs as he goes up to his death, a painting turned to hide something, to hide what? The painter that killed him, certainly.

—

In 1975, when Bacon was asked by David Sylvester why he had been painting so many self-portraits over the past few years, he could find nothing better to answer than: '. . . really because people have been dying around me like flies and I've nobody else left to paint but myself.' John Deakin had indeed died in 1972, but Bacon had never painted him, and though Dyer had died in 1971, Bacon was still painting him as frenziedly as he painted himself; as for Muriel Belcher, Isabel Rawsthorne, Henrietta Moraes, and Lucian Freud, his main models in the late 1960s, they were all alive and well. When I pointed this out to Manuela Mena, she simply laughed: 'Of course Bacon lied all the time. He was a dandy, and dandies are liars by definition.' He lied because he didn't want people to be too quick to see the obvious: that his paintings tell stories, fiendishly intelligent and enigmatic stories, and stories so intimate that often probably even he couldn't admit to himself how the naked truth of his being had suddenly been projected up there in a bright controlled splash of paint for all to see. Of course, they do not tell these stories in words, or in a way that can be translated into words, but in paint. And being told in paint they need to be read in paint. The stubborn lies also served this purpose: to prevent the viewer from relying on Bacon for an explanation, to force him or her to abandon the very idea of an explanation, and instead to turn to the paintings and patiently learn how to read them. Manuela Mena knows this very well, but the temptation sometimes still runs strong. In front of another one of his paintings, his 1965 *Crucifixion* perhaps, she sighs: 'I would so deeply love to have Bacon here, to explain some of these things to me, to confirm that I see what I see.' – 'There would be no point,' I answer. 'He could never tell you anything about his pictures that you couldn't see for yourself. He could no more read them for you than you can.' – 'Yes, but he knew things I don't, about how he made them, what he was thinking when he made them and then what changed along the way.' – 'It doesn't matter. What's there now is there, no matter what he thought, or thought he thought, or didn't think. And anyhow even if he did know something important, he wouldn't tell you; if your questions got close to the heart of the matter, he would just lie or get angry, as you know. Commentary is useless. The thing is there, and must be read as it exists, even when it is built to escape all understanding, or to trap it.'

Reading paintings, however, has its rules, and the first one is that nothing in the painting can be ignored. Earlier in the day Manuela Mena had insisted on this point: every single mark you see in a painting has been put there by the painter. This sounds obvious, but it is often forgotten when paintings are interpreted. Of course, there are accidental marks, flicks, drips, inherent to the 'fluid and curious' nature of oil painting, although often the painter uses and exploits those accidental marks too, even provokes them as Bacon so systematically did. But every single object you see in a painting, no matter how odd or insignificant or inexplicable (the safety pin in the curtain in the 1949 *Study from the Human Body*, the odd shadowy blob at the base of the right-hand panel of the 1962 *Three Studies for a Crucifixion*, the circle around the elbow of the central figure of the 1971 *Triptych – In Memory of George Dyer*) has been placed there, has been painted in, and thus, like Francesco del Cossa's snail or Georges de la Tour's wart, must be read when one attempts to read the painting. Sometimes, the painter obviously knew what he was doing, such as when Bacon hid a monochrome pope in his 1952 *Study for Crouching Nude*. I noticed it quite by accident: as Manuela Mena and I tried to look at another early painting, we were rather rudely pushed aside by a member of a French film crew, who was setting up lights to film this painting; as I stepped back, she shoved her lamp right in front of the *Crouching Nude*, and the light fell on it in such a way that, glancing at it sideways, I suddenly saw this Pope, floating in the striated space to the right of the canvas. When you look at the canvas under a normal light, straight on, or at a reproduction, you simply see a gray blur there, directly above a black blob; but if you crouch and look up, you can distinctly make out the face, the eyes and the mouth of the figure, easily identifiable as a pope by his high rounded cap and the downwards curving lines of his mozzetta, all painted in gray, in just a few strokes. The white caged framing device clearly indicates that this Pope is facing the crouching figure, the ostensible 'subject' of the painting, and his presence gives a whole new meaning to the crouch, it is a crouch of submission, the naked servant before his master, the naked child before his father. It was not an afterthought, nor an earlier version imperfectly painted out, and Bacon, who at the time was still feeling his way around and to the best of my knowledge never repeated this particular trick, did once later on implicitly allude to it: 'In the *Study for Crouching Nude* I tried to make the shadows as much *there* as the image. In a funny way, and though I hate the word, our shadows are our ghosts.'

Most of the time, however, Bacon was simply acting on instinct, or blindly following the dictates of his unconscious, as you prefer, without seeking to understand what a given detail meant, or at least only coming to understand it later, when the time came to reinterpret it. In the 1944 *Three Studies*, the right-hand leg of the curious wooden tripod set in front of the central hermaphroditic figure is extended by two curved pieces of wood, joined at the top by a little ball or knob; but whereas the rest of the wood of the tripod is painted in, albeit roughly, this rising extension, whose purpose remains mysterious to me but whose curve points directly to the phallic buttocks of the figure, is simply sketched in, deliberately and inexplicably left unfinished. 'Yes,' agrees Manuela Mena in front of the painting. 'I wish I could understand that.' The shape of this odd extension echoes an earlier Picasso-inspired organic figure, the dancing many-limbed nude in *Studio Interior* (painted circa 1934), one of whose appendages, to the right, has very much the same outline, and, raised in front of a blank canvas, remains equally unfinished. But Bacon painted this object again, at the very end of his life, and again altered it: in the 1988 *Second Version of Triptych 1944*, a faithful yet carefully modified reworking of the original triptych, the two curved pieces of wood, which are now joined by a bolt, are finished, painted all the way to the top. The shining metal bolt is what first caught my attention. 'Maybe he just put it there,' I first proposed to Manuela Mena, 'because he finally painted in the extension, and thus he had to bolt it together.' – 'Yes, perhaps. It's he himself who's finished. He's about to die.' That may be it, or then again it may not be; looking more closely, a little later, at the 'wooden knob' in the 1944 version, it appeared to me as an unfinished metal bolt; and one should also take into account the little metal plate fixed with two screws into the flesh of the biomorph in the 1988 reworking, right at the juncture of body and neck. It's the sort of plate one uses to repair something broken: but what is broken here? Bacon himself? He wouldn't undergo his kidney operation till the following year, but maybe the sense of falling apart, of needing to be cobbled back together, was already strong in him. Be that as it may, it isn't too hard to read the mysterious tripod, taken, who knows, from a dream, or some distant childhood memory, clearly associated with painting in any case (it reappears one last time, even more precisely depicted, in a 1991 portrait of his friend the painter Anthony Zych), as another 'emblem of painting', raw and unfinished as Bacon takes his first unsure steps into his art, perfectly, lovingly rendered as he is about to take his last bow and *filer à l'anglaise*, as the French say.

—

Having spent some six hours showing me the basic elements of Bacon's grammar and syntax, and pointing out to me the relations between his pictorial language and that of his great predecessors, it was only when she was called off to another appointment that Manuela Mena finally left me. 'May I stay?' I asked. – 'Of course!' she answered, outdoing in this final gesture her already excessive generosity. The guards had forgotten about me, and I remained alone. Most undemocratically, this is how these paintings (probably any painting) should be seen: alone in a great empty gallery, where the only sound is that of your heels on the wooden floor, where you can roam from one picture to the other whichever way your eye takes you, moving as close or as far as you like, or where, pulling up a chair, you can just sit your-self at the point of distance and look. Shuttling thus back and forth from picture to picture, taking the time to track the mutations of the imagery, their meaning will slowly rise and surround you; this is when the paintings will begin to talk to you, in a voice to my ear not unlike Macbeth's, in those lines Bacon loved so much:

> To-morrow, and to-morrow, and to-morrow,
> Creeps in this petty pace from day to day
> To the last syllables of recorded time,
> And all our yesterdays have lighted fools
> The way to dusty death. Out, out, brief candle!
> Life's but a walking shadow, a poor player,
> That struts and frets his hour upon the stage,
> And then is heard no more. It is a tale
> Told by an idiot, full of sound and fury,
> Signifying nothing.

Of course, the images will say something different to every person who looks at them, each will hear what he or she wants to hear from them, will see what he or she wants to see in them. That is what Bacon both ar-dently craved yet instantly swept from his mind, at the moment when, alone in his studio, paintbrush poised in hand, he bent toward the blank canvas; the act that his paintbrush accomplished then was the only one that mattered to him, a mysterious blending of his will, his science, his desire, his freedom and of chance, a pure act – one that produced either a disaster, or a painting.

– The Grammar of Francis Bacon –

IX

'I think that it is very difficult to talk about painting
. . . Painting is a world of its own, it is self-sufficient.
Most of the time when one talks about painting, one
says nothing interesting. It's always rather superficial.
What can one say? Basically, I believe that you simply
can't talk about painting, it just isn't possible.'
– Francis Bacon, April 1992

'Painting doesn't only show, it thinks.'
– Hubert Damisch

F rancis Bacon was a man keenly conscious of the
futility of all human endeavor, of the fragility
of flesh, of the tenuous and contingent quality of the
most intense emotions, of the infernal violence soak-
ing through the daily fiber of life. 'The simple fact of
being born is a very ferocious thing,' he believed, following in this Sophocles and Madame du Deffand; but
painting, for him, was not a protest against anything,
it was just a way of dealing with getting through the
days, the best and most fascinating way there was, as
well as, more secretly though put up there for all to see,
a way of unloading his most intimate ghosts. Painting
was a way of giving a material form, in the medium of

oil paint, to the vast meaninglessness pervading all of life, a meaninglessness that without this daily activity would have eventually overwhelmed him and drowned him. 'The important thing for a painter is to paint and nothing else,' he told Michel Archimbaud shortly before he died. Not that it necessarily had to be painting, it just worked out that way for him, ever since the day, before he even turned twenty, when he saw a Picasso exhibit and decided that this was what he would like to do. He took his time; he would be nearly forty before he began painting in earnest, and nearly sixty before he produced his greatest work. In this work he poured everything he had in him: his endless grief at life, his love of skin and flesh and colour, his frailty and his desires and his guilt, his rage and his incoherent longings. People found them horrific, though he insisted he never tried to be horrific. 'You can't be more horrific than life itself,' he threw in on one occasion. He was just reaching for the violence of reality; but as T. S. Eliot once wrote, 'Human kind cannot bear very much reality.' From the very start his paintings provoked incomprehension and misunderstanding, as well as very brutal rejection. As John Russell writes in his seminal 1971 study *Francis Bacon*, the reception of the *Three Studies for Figures at the Base of a Crucifixion*, first shown in early April 1945 at the Lefevre Gallery in London, was remarkably negative: 'They caused a total consternation. . . . They were regarded as freaks, monsters irrelevant to the concerns of the day, and the product of an imagination so eccentric as not to count in any possible permanent way.' Yet that same month Lee Miller entered the concentration camp at Dachau, and the terrifying photographs she published should have shown Bacon's viewers the immediate relevance of his images to the experience of life – and death – that millions of Europeans were then still undergoing every day. The postwar lull of course simply reinforced the criticism; in 1946, Bacon's paintings were castigated as 'alarming, distorted, sinister', and his first one-man show in 1949, which included his initial Velázquez pope image *Head VI*, was, as Martin Harrison remarks in his *In Camera*, 'greeted as "repellent," "violent" and "nightmarish." . . . The critical thrust fixed at that time,' he concludes, 'has by no means entirely subsided.' Even the British writer John Berger, one of the most sensitive art critics of the last fifty years, dismissed Bacon as a 'conformist' artist, infamously comparing him to Walt Disney. In America, where abstract expressionism long dominated the critical field, the rejection was even more categorical: Bacon's 1975 retrospective at the Metropolitan Museum of Art led the *New York Times*'s Hilton Kramer to conclude: 'In the world where M. Bacon's paintings are seen and bought and judged and talked about, to be avowedly homosexual, to traffic in images of sexual violence and personal sadism, is a good deal less shocking than, say, to be avowedly Methodist.' None of all this seemed to bother Bacon much, however: 'The way people regard my work is not my problem, it's their problem. I don't paint for others, I make paintings for myself.' Indeed, whatever it was these paintings were saying, they were saying it to him first; he painted to understand certain things, not to tell us things he already knew; for if he already knew them, then there was no need to paint them; no need to set the paint to thinking, thinking these things through for him. To read painting, as Hubert Damisch suggests, you not only have to look at what it shows you, you have to see how it thinks.

—

Shortly after the *Three Studies*, in 1946, Francis Bacon painted a large picture still simply known as *Painting*, one of his strangest ever, which combined in its imagery meat carcasses, drawn shades in a rounded room, a raised stage with microphones and swags, and a man in a suit with a savage open mouth, the upper half of his face hidden under a black umbrella. As Bacon later explained it, 'I was attempting to make a bird alighting on a field. And . . . suddenly the lines that I'd drawn suggested something totally different, and out of this suggestion arose this picture. I had no intention to do this picture; I never thought of it in that way. It was like one continuous accident mounting on top of another.' The open umbrella seems to have derived from the bird, possibly an umbrella bird, as Martin Harrison suggests. Harrison, who calls the umbrella 'a staple of Surrealist phallic symbolism', notes that Bacon had used it twice in the previous year, and relates it to 'numerous photographs of Hollywood film crews of the 1920s, in which an umbrella to shield the camera was a standard piece of equipment.' In an earlier painting, *Figure Study II* (itself a reworking of *Figure Study I*), a nude person, presumably male, proffers its buttocks, chastely draped however under a man's herringbone tweed coat; the umbrella looms over its shoulders, while a bit farther on, a mouth, not quite attached to the body, gasps in surprised pleasure (or distress?), the upper half of its face also missing, though not precisely hidden by the umbrella's shadow. Twenty-five years after the original, Bacon reprised *Painting*, simplifying it but keeping the umbrella, now beige. The umbrella had already reappeared in his work, however, the previous year, in 1970, framing the upper body of a headless naked female figure in the central panel of *Triptych–Studies of the Human Body*. And he would return to it again in his *Triptych 1974–1977* where it figures twice, on each of the side panels, again shading two male figures; while the one on the left has buried his head in the umbrella, the one on the right, for the very first time in this long series, shows his face, that of Bacon's dead lover George Dyer, his eyes closed. The umbrella would return one last time – if I am not mistaken – in a 1978 *Seated Figure*: this time, the figure's face is again obscured under the umbrella, showing only the nose and lower jaw; at its feet, a bust or a cut-out picture rises from the bottom of the canvas, the straightforwardly depicted profile of, once again, George Dyer,. The role or function of this ubiquitous umbrella, its persistent recurrence and its variations, the complex grammar of its associations seems to me to ask an interesting question. Why does it keep imposing itself thus to the painter, and to us?

Most viewers, looking at a painting by Francis Bacon, assume, without thinking as it were, that the human or animal figure before them is the subject of this picture. Yet that is not quite it: the figure is the painted *object* in the picture; the subject, as in all painting, not only abstract painting, is paint itself. It is the paint that talks about what it is about. 'Painting', as Bacon explained to Franck Maubert at some point in the 1980s, 'is a language in itself, it's a foreign tongue.' As such, it has its phonology (value and tonal relations) and its morphology (the disposition of form on the canvas), its grammar and its syntax, whose specific organization and articulation, in each painter's work, is the only thing that can teach you how to read that work. A careful study of the objects is of course crucial, and the large body of work that has emerged on the sources of Bacon's work has proven, like any iconological approach, a powerful tool, even if it rapidly reaches its limits, as Harrison's puzzled response to the black umbrella shows. For Bacon's grammar and his syntax must be read on their own, according to their own logic and their own laws. Not symbolically or metaphorically: Bacon was far too clever for that, and his paintings are crammed with deliberate traps and dead ends. It would be better to reason in terms of the classical Freudian operations, condensation, displacement, substitution, reversal, deformation, etc., or to refer to rhetorical figures such as metonymy or synecdoche; for it is also, to a certain extent, a question of rhetoric. It would also be better to decline to take too literally Bacon's pronouncements on the subject, his *official line* as it were, and simply to pay attention to what he himself called his 'technical imagination'. Above all, it would be better never to ask, 'What did Bacon mean to say here?' for not even he really knew that, but rather: 'What is the painting, here, telling us?' Take the time to really look at them, whether alone in a gallery or in the midst of a crowd glued to its audiphones, or even sitting in front of reproductions in a catalog or on a computer screen; look at them for a long time, moving back from one to another, patiently: little by little, you will begin to see how the paint is thinking.

Take, for instance, a minor example to begin with, the brutal (and rather unsuccesful) 1987 *Triptych*, three images framed in narrow pale rectangles themselves set on a background of velvety sand and vivid orange, which Bacon reportedly based on the García Lorca poem on the death of the bullfighter Ignacio Sánchez Mejías. The left-hand panel shows us the naked bullfighter's legs, lying sideways on a table, with a gaping wound on his thigh (precisely in Scarpa's triangle, an

41

area near the testicles where bullfighters are commonly gored while going in for the kill) circled in blue and designated by a red arrow; in the central panel, the naked bullfighter, his left knee bandaged, is standing, climbing a step, but again only his legs and genitals are depicted, with the bleeding wound placed just above, inset in a separate circle; and in the third, right-hand panel, we see a stylized bull's head and shoulders, one horn bloodied, under an unidentifiable bird- or batlike figure we can relate to Bacon's Erinyes figures in other canvases. Why is this creature lurking here? you might ask, what is its function? In my view, nothing forces us to read it as a symbol of the bullfighter's tragic destiny, of the vengeance wreaked by the bull for all its murdered brethren; on the contrary, we could take it as an indication that perhaps the painting is not at all about the bull and the wound it has inflicted, as we would first like to think, and are even dutifully informed by the little label pinned next to the work. Again, we must look at the paint itself and how it is applied. In the left panel, then, we might notice that the 'wound' in the sexless figure's thigh is shaped just like a vulva, a bleeding vulva (and what, also, are the two tassels or lamp cords, which Bacon always associates with bedrooms, doing in what is presumably an operating room?); and the wound in the central panel, very clearly and explicitly, is no wound at all, but rather a woman's breast, leaking blood from its nipple, rather than milk. If we then relate these facts to the single bloody horn, we might come to think that while this painting may well be 'about' the violence of combat between men and bulls, it is painted in such a way that it is also, if not mainly, about the violence of sex between men and women – an act that Bacon claimed he had only experienced once, not that one should accept his claims at face value. 'Painting tends towards a complete interlocking of image and paint,' he wrote in a 1953 tribute to the British painter Matthew Smith, 'so that the image is the paint and vice versa. Here the brushstroke creates the form and does not merely fill it in. Consequently, every movement of the brush on the canvas alters the shape and implications of the image. That is why real painting is a mysterious and continuous struggle with chance.' He couldn't have been clearer: again, the question is not what the painter *meant*: it is what the paint he applied *says*.

—

Because the images circulate from canvas to canvas, each time altered, modified, mirrored, distorted, it becomes necessary, in reading them, to track their displacements, frenzied or lazy, to look for the correspondences, the recurrent figures of this language or this rhetoric. Many have already been discussed by those who have studied Bacon. The mouth, for instance, Bacon's fantastic gaping mouths, which he wanted to paint 'like Monet painted water lilies (or sunsets)'; everything, or nearly, has been written about these mouths, how they were inspired by the screaming nurse in Eisenstein's *Battleship Potemkin*, by a book of hand-coloured plates of diseases of the mouth, by the howling mother in Poussin's *Massacre of the Innocents* ('The best human cry in painting,' said Bacon); how they evoke a screech of anguish, a moan of pleasure, or the frantic gasping of a lifelong asthmatic, such as he was. Martin Harrison even briefly cites a 1930 article by George Bataille, published in his magazine *Documents*, which Bacon was known to read at the time. Entitled simply 'Mouth', it's worth quoting at length, for Bacon would certainly have recognized his own obsessions in this text:

The mouth is the beginning, or, if you will, the prow of animals . . . the most alive part, meaning the most terrifying for neighboring animals. But man does not have a simple architecture like beasts, and it is not possible to say just where he begins . . . it is his eyes or his forehead that play the role of signification of the jaw of animals.

Looking at the way the tooth-filled mouths, in Bacon's early paintings especially, conclude a long, thrusting or craning neck or are sometimes set vertically, prolonging the body upward, we cannot help but think of this Bataillian mouth, which in the 'distressed individual . . . comes to place itself inasmuch as possible in the prolongation of the spinal column, meaning in the position it normally occupies in the animal constitution.' This, indeed, is probably a key to what gives some of Bacon's mouths, no matter how improbably positioned, their feeling of inevitability.

After the mouths, the eyes, their presence or their absence. If we except a few early paintings he repudiated or destroyed, it seems that Bacon didn't paint eyes till 1949, in his *Head III*; before that, he usually just paints the lower half of the face (all the 1946 paintings, or most of the other 1949 *Heads*, including *Head VI*, his first pope); and if the top of the head is represented, it is either turned away (*Study from the Human Body* 1949), or covered, as in the *Three Studies* by the hair of the left-hand figure or the bandages of the central figure. All of this tells us rather directly that we should be paying attention to these eyes, painted or not, as well as to the direction of their gaze. As time goes on, Bacon will work his way through every conceivable variation on the eye: the straight, frontal gaze, inaugurated by the 1950 pope; the use of glasses or spectacles, often crushed (*Pope I*, 1951); closed eyes (as in his first 1956 *Self-Portrait*, or the 1955 *Study for a Portrait II* based on William Blake's life mask, and of course the eyes of George Dyer in all the portraits painted after his death); sockets with no eyes (the awesome figure, squirming in an ecstasy of agony, in the central panel of the 1962 *Three Studies for a Crucifixion*); the single eye in profile (so many of the 1960s George Dyers); the single eye facing, both open and closed (the 1976 *Triptych*, where the right eye of both the 'Hitler' and the 'Mussolini' figures disappears under an oval blob); and many more still. These variations are never purely formal, they have a precise meaning in each painting, at every stage of the artist's development. With his two baldly narrative 1960s Crucifixions, Bacon introduced the figure of the 'indifferent witness', one that either looks away from the other's suffering or glances at it without caring; this figure too will reappear at specific moments, strategically and hauntingly imposing its indifference on the scene being played out on the canvas. And after the suicide of his lover George Dyer in 1971, it'll be four years before he can paint clear open eyes again, eyes looking straight at the viewer (the first will be those of Peter Beard, in 1975); for more than a decade the dead Dyer's eyes remain tightly shut, as most often do the painter's own, repeating from one portrait to the next: 'I can't look at this.'

In 1988, Bacon reprised his 1944 *Three Studies*: like Glenn Gould re-recording in 1981 his inaugural 1955 *Goldberg Variations* (trading, at fifty-one minutes instead of thirty-seven, his youthful exuberance and brio for the serene perfection of pure mathematics, of limpid, nearly abstract sound), the painter, sensing death is near, revisits the moment of his birth as an artist, to show (to himself?) how far he has come, and like the pianist willingly sacrifices the crude harshness, the pulsing raw anger and the savage energy of the original for a grand lyrical elegance, somber, voluptuous, and above all painterly. There are important modifications, a few of which he acknowledged, others more discrete: the colour of the background, of course, the proportion of the figures in relation to the canvas (their actual size hardly differs), the lower body of the right-hand figure. On the left-hand female figure, otherwise very much an exact replica of the original, he introduced a remarkable though barely noticeable change: the head is now ever so slightly raised, and an eye socket, if not an eye, appears from under the mass of hair; the figure, it now seems, is *looking* at something, the figure in the central panel if we want to read it that way; in any case looking. And with Bacon, the gaze is never innocent (nothing ever is, in fact).

—

That Bacon's images always constitute enigmas seems to me inevitable. Hans Belting, formulating his anthropology of images, explains it thus: the image, an answer to the enigma of death, uncovers a new enigma in the image. It helps, as I have suggested, to confront the different enigmas. In the classical art historian tradition, you read each painting on its own, by itself. Of course, every painting is connected to others through the iconography it deploys, which the scholar can identify and analyze, both in its general significance and in the way the painting under consideration treats it. But the problem with Bacon is that he self-generates his iconography, pulling it from a vast repertoire of sources and playfully subverting everything he touches. When depicting himself in paint, he did so in two distinct manners: representationally, as a man nearly always clothed, characterized by his foppish forelock even when the features are utterly distorted; and figuratively as a hermaphroditic creature, blurring the distinction between his 'male' and his 'female' nature, embodying how for him, psychically speaking, his sex was not a condition but a state (Bataille: '*Le sexe est un état*'). Like the toy dinosaurs scattered throughout Nobuyoshi Araki's photographs, the hermaphrodite is Bacon's secret signature, the painter's emblem in the painting. The first of these numerous hermaphrodites is certainly the central figure of the 1944 *Three Studies* (the one the left-hand female figure may or may not be peering at from under her hair, as the 1988 version suggests). It is perched on the sort of narrow wooden tripod used for old film cameras, or perhaps an easel – in any case something to make images with. In front of it, the painter has placed another, shorter tripod, but a rather odd one, with a strange curved addition, made of two pieces of wood joined at their tip by a bolt, rising up from one of the legs. Casually left unfinished in the 1944 version, it is lovingly rendered in the 1988 one. I have not been able to identify it, and Philippe Comar, a French art historian who is also a specialist of measuring instruments, assures me that 'there exists no painter's or sculptor's instrument to which this thing directly refers. However, given the repetition of the object in several paintings, and given the

48

fact that Bacon always used objects he had at hand, it must indeed exist. . . . If Bacon,' he adds in his letter, 'went to the trouble of making this rickety tripod unidentifiable, raising it to the dignity of a pure idea, this means that we must make do with it, and that nothing further can be granted us.' I can go no further, other than to repeat what I have already asserted elsewhere, that this singular tripod clearly functions as an emblem of painting, of painting in general; which confirms that the central biomorph of the triptych, the hermaphroditic biomorph, can indeed be identified as a form of self-portrait. And whereas Bacon never, to the best of my knowledge, re-employed the little tripod between the two versions of the *Three Studies*, it must have stuck in his head after he dragged it out of the attic of memory, dusted it off, and repainted it, because soon after, in 1991, he placed it once again in front of a portrait of his friend Anthony Zych, a minor painter. This time, however, a little white object lies on top of the tripod, a notched strip of paper bearing an arrow, which to me looks exactly like the ticket one draws at the butcher shop or the post office to wait one's turn. Our interpretation of its exact meaning, here, will depend both on our knowledge of the nature of Bacon's relationship to Zych and our appreciation of his character. If one is of a generous bent, one could understand it as saying to Zych: 'Your turn will come.' Those of us with a more pessimistic view of human nature in general, and of Bacon's in particular,

X

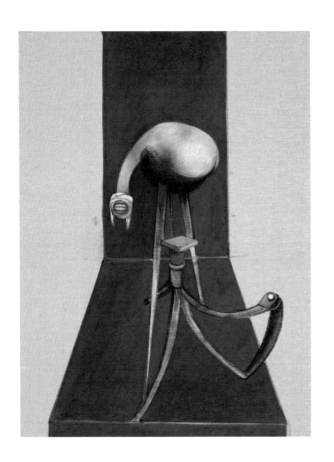

XI

XII

might however be inclined to read: 'You want to be a painter, mate? Get on line.'

The problem is further complicated by the fact that the imagery circulates from one painting to the next not just in terms of the objects depicted, transformed or not, but also through other elements, such as the background colour or the framing devices. Two different paintings can be placed in relation to each other through the reappearance of the same figure; in the same way, two different figures can be put in relation through the reappearance of a given colour, or of a similar framing device (we know that Bacon worked near a wall covered with photographs of his previous paintings, and often painted in series). Let us return to our whining, threatened, blindfolded hermaphroditic creature. In 1988, it is set on a red-draped rostrum very similar to the one upon which rises the central figure of the 1981 *Triptych Inspired by the Oresteia of Aeschylus*, a figure bearing to the sacrifice, in the libation cup, its own reversed and eyeless head. This latter figure is usually identified as Agamemnon, stepping on the crimson cloth treacherously laid out by Clytemnestra as he heads to his death, framed between his avenger Orestes on the right panel (who is, curiously, about to pass the same door as all those Dyers about to die) and a dangling batlike Erinyes on the left one ('Sybil at Cumae in cage clinging upside down like a sloth,' Bacon jotted on a scrap of blue airmail paper, alluding to the line from the *Satyricon* used by T. S. Eliot as an epigraph to *The*

Waste Land: 'For I myself once saw with my own eyes the Cumaean Sibyl hanging in a cage [or a jar, according to some translations], and when some boys asked her: *Sibyl, what do you want?* she answered: *I want to die*.'). Yet this putative Agamemnon is also a replica of the central figure of the 1976 *Triptych*, where it appears not mounting a podium but rather emerging from or even painted on a thick panel or stack of canvases, though already bearing its own head toward a fount overflowing with blood (or, why not? with red paint), while a flock of vultures (perhaps the same vultures devouring the liver of Tityos, that double of Prometheus, in the paintings by Titian and Ribero) attack its shoulders; furthermore, as is made explicit by a 1982–1984 *Diptych* based on Ingres, these rounded shoulders can also be read as breasts, designating this voluntary sacrificial victim not as the murdered father of the Atreides cycle but as one more hermaphroditic double of Bacon himself. This relationship between these three central panels (four, if you count the 1944 version of the *Three Studies*, retroactively dragged into this sad story) operates through rigorous permutations, and thus in turn mechanically brings into play the three (or four) sets of side panels. Without going any further, one at the very least might be willing to conclude that if the painter at first depicted himself as little Francis, the childish or naked submissive figure crouching in fear before various overbearing and often raging popes, Nazi goons, or sundry other paternal figures, things changed over time; and as Francis became Bacon, and grew rich and famous and powerful, and more and more isolated as well, he slowly came to occupy the place of *il papa* himself, caged, trapped, petrified in his grandeur. The last pope paintings show this openly. In 1954, already, the setting of *Figure with Meat*, another pope, was directly inspired by a John Deakin photograph of Bacon sitting in front of two hanging carcasses; by 1962, the pope, alone in a concave blood red room, is squirming in anguish on his throne, his legs crossed in the pose Bacon usually strikes in his self-portraits, as he often did in life. And when he repainted his signature figure for the last time, in 1971 as a *Study for Red Pope – Second Version*, the setting has kept the same overall design but has now become a hall of funhouse mirrors, in which the awkwardly positioned painter-pope gazes glumly, not at his own reflection but at a defiant man in a suit, waving a threatening fist yet stubbornly refusing to open his eyes and look at him. Self-sacrifice might then become the only way out of such a quandary, the laying of one's head at the feet of the lover-son, whom one can nonetheless never cease painting, and thus murdering too.

It is not clear exactly when Bacon perceived this, but by 1971, the year he painted that last pope, his painting knew it with a cold, furious certainty. The *Pope* had been made especially for the great Bacon retrospective at the Grand Palais in Paris, along with a matching *Study of George Dyer* in which his lover, nearly naked, is represented in the same position as the pope and in an almost identical setting; yet unlike the pope the Dyer figure keeps his eyes shut, and the mirror has pivoted away, showing only part of his leg; the two pictures, it should be added, were not hung together, the Dyer, instead, being presented as a diptych together with a female nude under a shower, a naked baby crawling towards her (Bacon later destroyed this painting, in effect returning this Dyer to his pope). The night before the retrospective opened, after a violent row that ended with Bacon moving to a friend's room, George Dyer killed himself in their hotel bathroom, leaving the painter alone with his canvases, his brushes, his colours and his merciless gaze. What could he do but paint more, work his way out of the pit in paint? A month later he began the *Triptych – In Memory of George Dyer*, the first of a great series of works made in response to his lover's suicide. I believe that to read this painting you need to look at it together with an earlier one, painted a year before Dyer's death, the 1970 *Triptych – Studies of the Human Body*. In these three simple but intensely powerful canvases, three female figures are set against a beautiful pale lavender background (the same lavender, a bit lighter perhaps, that serves as background for the 1971 Dyer triptych), a flat even plane broken only by a long curving beam structure, running in a nearly uninterrupted arc through all three paintings. The middle figure, headless, sits on a board (possibly a diving board) under one of the inevitable black umbrellas; its female sex is explicitly painted as a thick black triangle (which I would be glad to read as a pictorial nod to the one placed, for similar reasons no doubt, by Petrus Christus between the folds of the dress of his pale chaste 1470 *Young Lady*). Bacon's figure is anything but chaste; its hanging breasts, its generous hips and its swarthy pubis are made for sex; once again, the headless shoulders painted as a second set of breasts (the nipple is clearly visible on the left shoulder) suggest that, though it is directly drawn from a photograph of Henrietta Moraes, it might in fact serve, like the figures described above, as yet another double of Bacon, a nearly fully female one this time. What is the umbrella doing there, then? I don't have an easy answer for the umbrella; sitting on my sunlit terrace after lunch trying to read an essay on Brueghel, annoyedly shifting my chair to keep my head in the shade of a large parasol while still warming my legs in the sun, I suddenly wondered if it wasn't just about keeping the head in the dark. Whether or not we agree with the umbrella's association with the early making of film, and thus with the making of images, we need to read it together with the systematic blindness of the figures caught under it, a blindness most often pictorially generated by the umbrella itself or its shadow, black paint cancelling the figure's eyes; and I would thus choose to see in it, rather than a phallic symbol, a figure of death, the death the painter is constantly struggling with in his painting (Bachelard: 'Death is first an image, and it remains an image'), the death that the painter visits upon his images in painting them, especially when he is painting himself; the death that paint visits upon the painter. The figure to the left kneels on the beam, but as if with its back completely twisted so that its head hangs upside down, its long hair trailing and its breasts pointing straight up; as for the figure to the right, it has been convincingly related by David Sylvester to Caravaggio's 1597–1599 *Narcissus*, 'undressed and regendered' as Martin Harrison puts it (and with the left shoulder altered, echoing the shoulder/breasts of the two other figures); the male head and especially the bold forelock clearly once again mark it as a self-representation. The painter as Narcissus, then, and a Narcissus slowly dying in paint, is the subject of the entire triptych; an interpretation confirmed by the fact that when this entranced, tormented, or lustful her-maphrodite gazes down into the pool of pale lavender paint, he/she/it, unlike in the Ovidian myth or in the Caravaggio, sees nothing, for as Bacon clearly under-stood – Bacon who of course knew his Alberti – the reflection is not in the pool, but in the painting.

The reuse of the lavender background and the curved beam is what first links the 1971 Dyer triptych to the 1970 one, and thus to the myth of Narcissus, or rather of the painter as Narcissus. The impression is strengthened by the resemblance of the pose of the figures in the two left-hand panels: but in 1971, the twisted female has been repainted as a collapsing male

XIII

XIV

XV

boxer, bleeding and battered, knocked down by the white ball coming to a rest on the pale yellow-purple blob flowing out of his arm. One of my friends believes that this object, painted with all the delicacy of the skin of a Velázquez infanta, might be a cricket ball, 'a strikingly modern image of death', bowled straight into the face of Dyer the Proletarian Boxer Hero by his more aristocratic lover-painter, with the same precision and violence as he flung all those little white balls of paint at Dyer in so many other canvases, including the right-hand panel of this triptych. This latter appears very different from the one in the 1970 triptych: above the curved beam, now, is set a profiled portrait of Dyer, doubled this time by a reflection, cast not, however, in Narcissus's pool but in a square mirror that is also a table, within which the mirror image lies reversed, like the heads on a playing card (Bacon the gambler, always playing his card games, but on the mute and resigned face of his lover rather than on smooth green baize). In the central panel, finally, which, except for two areas of lavender background, bears no overt pictorial connection at all to the one in the 1970 triptych, 'George Dyer', his head in shadow, opens a door with a key and starts up the stairs toward the Paris hotel room where he will meet his death; behind the banister, in a corner, looms a canvas turned to the wall, the edges of its stretcher catching the light. Its painted surface is invisible to us, but of course we know what's on it, thanks to the glowing tassel and Velázquez's *Meninas*:

the self-portrait of the painter, as Narcissus, lover and murderer (in the 1970 triptych, it was the paint alone that killed the painter-Narcissus). Dyer's two profiles in the right-hand panel bring an additional element to this story: the right-side-up profile has its sole eye open, but looks to the right, out of the field of the triptych, away from the central scene and the one to the left; the bottom profile, which is turned towards the two scenes representing its fate, has its eye tightly shut. Once again, the paint says, 'I can't look at this.' Even when he was alive Dyer 'couldn't look at this'. In the 1968 *Two Studies for a Portrait of George Dyer*, the painted Dyer, nailed to the canvas, his redoubled face trying to rip itself off the surface, glares at the Dyer sitting on the chair, who, having smoked a great many cigarettes, looks away, turning his back to the raw suffering of his painted double; he is not, however, indifferent, rather he is pleading, his two hands cupped together, begging or offering something we are not shown, his wounded heart perhaps. The lover-object wants only one thing, for the painter to look at him: but the painter only looks at himself, as in the moving torn photograph of the two men, taken in Soho by John Deakin around 1964, where Bacon, proud, confident, and cocky, stares straight at the camera (at us, at himself), while Dyer shyly tries to look at him, unable as always to catch his gaze. At least that is how Bacon saw it, or at least how, in the anguished solitude of his studio, he painted it. In 1968 he made another

XVI

XVII

extraordinary picture of Dyer, a magnificent lyrical or-
chestration of blues and pale purples echoing the *Two
Studies*, a *Portrait of George Dyer in a Mirror* where
the sitting figure now does face the mirror, yet, painted
as a folded photograph, with a line straight through
its body, remains faceless; and the image in the mirror,
forever refusing to be the beloved double of Bacon-
Narcissus, looks away, its eyes tightly shut, its face torn
off its head, a reflection desperately trying not to be
one. It was Dyer's inability to impose himself before
Bacon's gaze as an individual to be loved rather than
as a double to be painted that drove him to his death,
Bacon seems to have concluded, and that was what he
furiously and frantically painted for several years after
Dyer's death, first once and then again, in 1972, in a
Triptych dated August where Dyer, to the left, stoically
keeps his eyes clamped shut as the black shadow of
death begins to swallow him up and, in a pink flood,
'the life flows out of him' (as Bacon put it to a friend),
while the figure on the right – which could once again
be Dyer (as suggested by the flowing pink and the white
underwear, the same the real Dyer wore in the Deakin
studio photos) just as easily as Bacon himself, as the
indifferent witness, narcissistically identified with his
lover – keeps its eyes closed too and turns its back to
the two naked figures violently copulating or wrestling
in the middle, the one on top viciously smashing the
bottom's ones face into the ground (in a gesture clearly
described by the curve of the white arrow); and then

yet again, several times, until at last, in May and June of 1973, he was able to paint Dyer's death just as it occurred, to describe it as a fact, a most brutal one perhaps, but a fact nonetheless. In this, one of his greatest paintings, imbued with an eerie stillness in spite of the violence of the event depicted, Dyer still dies with his eyes tightly shut; the shut eyes, like the turned back, have become the mark of death. Bacon must have felt so much sorrow and anger at this death, you can see it in the paintings, rage at Dyer for leaving him like that, pity, guilt of course; violent, conflicting emotions which he thought about in paint, and slowly came to understand in paint, the only language he truly knew.

—

Bacon was a gambler, a serious gambler; and the way he played with everything, people and images, in his life as in his art, was also dead serious (*serio ludere*, as they said during the Renaissance), yet wildly playful too, Bacon enjoying the game for what it was, no matter how high the stakes. His artistic credo, as he constantly repeated to his various interviewers, placed chance at the heart of his 'technical imagination' (which, as he explained to Marguerite Duras, 'is the instinct that works outside the rules to turn the subject back onto the nervous system with all the force of nature'). As soon as he thought he knew where he was going, he would change direction, to destabilize and ruin his certitudes, even at the risk of ruining the picture in the process, and himself. He approached his work with a passionate painterly intelligence but also a sort of low animal cunning, as if he was always trying to set a trap for himself, a trap out of which something unexpected would spring. He called this 'the will to lose one's will, to make oneself completely free.' To let the paint think for itself, he could have added. His canvases seem formally conceived as 'machine-paintings', a term first introduced by the French painter and theoretician Du Fresnoy in 1668, and commented on forty years later by Roger de Piles in the following terms: 'A machine is a precise assembly of several pieces working together to produce a single effect' (and therein differs from a mechanism). In Bacon's case, the effect of the pieces is to drag the viewer into the painting and submit him to what the picture *does*, just as it submitted its creator. But no painting was ever definitive, the Baconian machine had to be reset each time by the next painting, and each time the painter tottered on the brink, courting failure. When asked by Duras, in 1971, if he felt in danger of death when he painted, he tried to dodge the question by invoking another painter: 'I become very nervous,' he said. 'You know, Ingres would weep for hours before beginning a painting. Especially a portrait.' He knew the risks, and he also knew the fatigue, the fear, the failure of will or of intelligence or of imagination; when the painting went awry, he didn't hesitate to destroy it, no matter how good what he had ruined had once been. Then he would start again. He wanted 'every brushstroke to have the same energy as the first one', and knew just how difficult that was to achieve and just how magical it was when it did occur (talking about Van Gogh, he once said: 'His brushstrokes, at the end of his life, the strength of his brushstrokes, there is no explanation for that'). 'I don't think people understand how mysterious . . . the actual manipulation of oil paint is,' he commented on another occasion. He termed nearly everything he did a *Study*; had he ever signed his paintings, he could have done so like the best painters of antiquity, who, Pliny tells us, 'always placed on even finished works a suspensive inscription, such as *Apelles Faciebat* or *Polyclitus Pingebat* ['Apelles was making', 'Polyclitus was painting'] as if art was something always begun anew and always unfinished.' This was not, however, mere repetition, things constantly changed, evolved, mutated, and not just the manner or the style: the painting changed both what was painted and the painter himself. Bacon's last major painting is once again an unnamed triptych, painted not on canvas but on linen, as if it were his shroud. This time, there are only black squares on a beige background, black openings that two naked male figures, painted up to the waist, with no arms to wave good-bye with and no faces to weep, are stepping in or out of, calmly, confidently and without fear. In lieu of torsos and heads hang two painted portraits, depicted, with an unusually naturalistic realism, as if they were nailed onto the canvas: on the left, where the turn of the foot indicates the figure is stepping out of the black, the face is commonly identified as being that of the Brazilian race car driver Ayrton Senna, taken from a magazine cover, but if this is the case, it is standing in for that of José Capelo, a young Spaniard who became Bacon's protégé at the end of his life (and who looked much like Senna); on the right, the face is that of Bacon himself, a meticulous reproduction of a 1972 close-up photograph; the body below it, stepping into the black square, is once again, in spite of a small discrete penis, painted as ripely feminine. In the center, two figures are making love, in the same pose taken from the Muybridge images of wrestlers that Bacon had obsessively reworked since his beautiful 1953 *Two Figures* and its fabulously tender 1954 variation, *Two Figures in the Grass*. Whereas in the Dyer *Triptych – August 1972* the sex (or the struggle) was despairingly brutal, here it appears nearly loving: the movement of the black arrow now suggests that the figure on the bottom is turning its face, which we can't see, toward the face of the other figure; hidden in shadows, the two are looking at each other, perhaps even kissing, just as the two pinned portraits are looking straight at us, with a clear, open gaze. Narcissus, at last releasing his double out into life, is ready to step into death.

– The True Image –

XVIII

It might be thanks to the toilets at the Metropolitan Museum of Art, situated, for some odd reason, in the depths of the Egyptian art section, that I first had the idea of considering the paintings of Francis Bacon in the light of the Byzantine practice of images. I had come to the Met to see the Bacon retrospective, not Egyptian art; but the location of this bathroom forces you to wander a bit, past, among other marvels, a half-dozen beautiful little portraits, the famous Fayyum mummy paintings, which suddenly reached out, seized me, and drew me in. I knew these portraits, of course, I had seen them several times over the years, but I had never experienced them with this intensity. It was as if these long-dead men and women were abruptly present, as present as the people standing next to me, right here in this museum; as if their portraits somehow brought their vanished lives directly into my own. I looked at them for a long time. And then I went and found the men's room, and then I came back and looked at them some more, and then I went upstairs to see the Bacon show.

Later I found myself thinking about these portraits and about the sense of reality that emanates from them. It is a reality that has nothing to do with the reality of a Bacon painting. I read about them, and I learned a few things. I learned for instance that while some of them – such as, probably, the boy Eutyches, or the nameless thin-faced bearded man who gazed out at me with such sad, longing, living eyes – were paint- ed directly from the model, either before or just after death, most of them were turned out by craftsmen who had never set eyes on the deceased and who applied a few basic details supplied by relatives to standardized models, a template that bore no relation to the actual bone structure, revealed by X-rays, of the mummy. I also learned that these painters employed pictorial techniques, brought to Egypt by Greek colonists, that had been invented centuries before by the great Greek naturalist painters; yet while none of the ancient Greek works have survived, we have found, preserved by the dryness of the Egyptian climate, nearly a thousand of these mummy paintings, mute witnesses both to the lives of the dead and to a dead tradition. It was the tra- dition of Apelles, Alexander the Great's court painter, whom the ancients considered the most accomplished artist in history: we have Pliny's and Lucian's word for it, and a handful of Roman mosaic copies of his paintings, and nothing else. The techniques Apelles and his predecessors developed would probably have been lost altogether, along with their works, if at the time of the Roman occupation, in the first century AD, wealthy Egyptians hadn't gradually started replacing

XIX

the stylized masks covering the faces of their mummies with lifelike portraits painted on flat wooden boards, opening a whole new market for the painting skills struggling to stay alive in the Greek workshops of Alexandria. And so when the Christians finally came to accept painting, a few centuries later, the techniques would still be there for them to draw on, even as they altered their intent.

None of this tells us anything about the truth of these images. I am tempted to venture that they are in fact truthful rather than true; that thanks to their sometimes extraordinary realism, their marvellous mimetic recreation of the faces of the dead, they make the dead real for us, but as people, not as paintings. And this is probably also because they call upon reflexes of looking that are deeply ingrained in us. They are made, after all, in the same way as the pictures that we have been taught – here in the West – to regard as great painting: pictures made according to the logic, prevalent from Giotto to Courbet, of a sculptural imitation, in depth, of the subject. Even the first time we see a Fayyum portrait, it already looks familiar to us, as a painting. The features of the face, painted most often in encaustic (pigments mixed into melted wax, which must be applied very fast before it sets), are clearly contoured and defined in subtly-coloured flesh tints, using a technique, already fully worked out, of lighting and shadowing to provide the illusion of depth and roundness. The portrait of Eutyches, for instance, is visibly illuminated from the upper left and, like many of the others, is animated by delicate white highlights in the eyes and along the nose; the *contrapposto* of his shoulders, turned back to the right while the face gazes straight out at us, adds to the intensity of the sense of life conveyed by this portrait. It seems real to us because this is what we have been told for centuries to consider real. Pliny tells the same stories of Apelles – how his painted horse, for instance, looked so lifelike that it caused real horses to neigh – that his contemporaries told of Velázquez. '*Troppo vero!*' it is said Pope Innocent X exclaimed when he was first shown his portrait (the one Bacon would so obsessively repeat a few centuries later); and when Juan de Pareja, Velázquez's freed slave, was dispatched to show his recently finished portrait – portrait that has also ended up at the Metropolitan Museum – to his master's friends, their reaction, in the anecdote reported by his biographer Antonio Palomino, was 'to look at the painted portrait and at the original in awe and wonder, not knowing to whom they should speak or who would answer them'; when first shown in Rome in 1649, it 'was generally applauded by all the painters from different countries, who said that the other pictures [in the show] were art, but this one alone was truth.' Yet truth in painting is never a thing fixed once and for all.

Francis Bacon, whose paintings, when I saw them at the Metropolitan, hung a few rooms away from Velázquez's *Juan de Pareja*, Rembrandt's self-portraits, a handful of Vermeers, and Goya's mournful and luminous portrait of the young Don Manuel Osorio, desperately wanted to paint true paintings, paintings as true and as alive as any of these. At his most ambitious, he even dreamed of making 'the one picture which will annihilate all the other ones.' Of course there would always be another painting; but at his best – in his small portraits of the 1960s and 1970s, in the large paintings of his friends made in the second half of the 1960s, in the series of triptychs he painted after the death of his lover George Dyer – the images he has left us are images we immediately recognize as true images, perhaps even as some of the truest and strongest images of his century. What is more complicated is to define the nature of the truth in these pictures. It is a commonplace to say that since the arrival of photography, which rapidly took over the task, so long entrusted to painting, of representing the real, truth in painting could no longer be founded on illusion, on mimesis, and that painting, since Manet at least, has been forced to invent radically new means to express its truth. Yet still a part of us instinctively tends to identify truth in images with representational realism, as I had before the Fayyum portraits; and when we begin to talk of another form of pictorial truth, as we have for a century and a half now, we immediately reach for a vocabulary that is essentially religious, we talk about a 'higher' or a 'deeper' truth. Malraux deplored this fact: 'The religious vocabulary, here, is irritating, but no other exists.' Bacon however, over the course of his long life, sought to develop his own vocabulary to make these distinctions; for him, any work that simply sought to copy the real was now no more than 'illustration': what was needed, as he reads off from a scrap of paper in a 1985 filmed interview conducted by Melvyn Bragg, was 'not an illustration of reality, but to create images which are a concentration of reality and a shorthand of sensation.' He was, as we know, a deeply unreligious man. In a recent documentary about his life, we see him archly snapping at a hapless French journalist, who has just asked him if he believes in God: 'No! Why are you asking me such a stupid question?' This didn't prevent him from acknowledging the central importance of the Christian faiths to the history of Western images: 'One knows how very potent some of the images of Christianity have been,' he told David Sylvester in 1966, 'and how they must have played very deeply on one's sensibility. So one can never say that one has got completely away.' But his debt to Christian art went much further than crucifixions or popes, than the content of the Christian images he drew on; it is the nature of his idea of truth in painting, like ours, that is religious in essence. Because the fact is that in our culture it is the very idea that there might be such a thing as truth in images, that there are such things as true images, that is religious.

The Greeks, even as they made them, always remained wary of images; for centuries, Plato's critique

– if the things of this world are but shadows of their ideal form, what truth then could lie in images, which are but shadows of these shadows? – hung over the Greek painters like a sword of Damocles. Images, this is what I was suggesting about the Fayyum portraits, could at best be truthful, never true. And the early Christians, of course, were even more deeply skeptical than Plato and rejected images for their religion, invoking the Jewish prohibition and their own horror of the pagan worship of graven images: 'They be not gods, which are made with hands,' clamoured Paul, the former Pharisee (Acts 19:26). The first written mention of a Christian portrait, which appears in the second-century apocryphal Acts of John, is still strongly tinged with the Pauline suspicion (as well, probably, as the Platonic one): Lycomedes, a disciple of John, secretly has a portrait of his master painted so that he can worship it in his cell. But John

went into the bedchamber, and saw the portrait of an old man crowned with garlands, and lamps and altars set before it. And he called him and said: Lycomedes, what meanest thou by this matter of the portrait? can it be one of thy gods that is painted here? for I see that thou art still living in heathen fashion. . . . And Lycomedes answered him: . . . It is thou, father, whom I have had painted in that portrait. [. . .]

And John who had never at any time seen his own face said to him: Thou mockest me, child: am I like that in form, [excelling] thy Lord? how canst thou persuade me that the portrait is like me? And Lycomedes brought him a mirror. And when he had seen himself in the mirror and looked earnestly at the portrait, he said: As the Lord Jesus Christ liveth, the portrait is like me: yet not like me, child, but like my fleshly image. . . . This that thou hast now done is childish and imperfect: thou hast drawn a dead likeness of the dead, [instead of the likeness of the living in a living soul].

– Acts of John 27–29, translation by M. R. James, 1924

At the beginning of the fourth century, Eusebius of Caesarea would still be asking, in a letter to the emperor's sister Constantia Augusta, which of the two natures of the Man-God she thought to find in an image of Him? The divine nature, he argued, could not be represented, and as for the human one, there was no point in doing so. However the mass conversions that followed the conversion of Constantine in 312 AD were already bursting open the floodgates; soon images, spreading from the privacy of homes where they had never ceased to thrive, would begin to inundate the public and the religious space, the palaces, the monasteries, and the churches. The political and religious authorities, unable to stem the flood, had to adapt and were thus obliged to recognize that in relation to the Mosaic prohibition the coming of Jesus had altered the rules of the game. As Hans Belting writes in the book whose title I have borrowed, *The True Image*, 'God, [through his birth,] had finally shown himself in an image. Only this wasn't a made image, but a body. . . . Images, when finally they began to circulate, drew their

XX

authority first and foremost from this body. Those that later came to be designated as true were true inasmuch as they attested the true body of Christ.' Thus together with the earliest Christian icons arose the notion of the True Image; a crucial notion, as an image could only be permitted if it was true. And this idea was to take on a very specific form, or rather forms; from the start, there were to be, for the Christians, two kinds of True Images: the *Acheiropoieta,* or 'Images Not Made by Hands', and the Images of Saint Luke.

The concept of the 'Images Not Made by Hands' was a direct response to Paul's attack on the sculpted gods worshipped by the pagans. The prototype of these images is the famed *Mandylion* of Edessa, which was probably made in the sixth century: according to the image's legend, King Abgar V, desperately ill, had sent Christ a messenger, asking him to allow himself to be painted; Christ, in response, pressed his face into a cloth, where it imprinted his True Image. Brought to Constantinople in 944, the *Mandylion* seems to have passed into the hands of the king of France, Louis IX, in 1241, a few decades after the Latin conquest of the city, and to have remained in the Sainte Chapelle of Paris until 1792, when it finally vanished in the turmoil of the French Revolution. In the West, however, its fame had already long been eclipsed by another Acheiropoieton, the Veil of Veronica, also known as the *Vera Icona* or true icon, an image of Christ's face that had remained on the cloth Saint Veronica used to

wipe his sweat as he bore his cross to Calvary. These
and other similar Acheiropoieta (such as the Christ
of Camuliana, of which the Byzantine poet George
of Pisidia wrote: 'This unpainted painting, not made
by human hands', or, closer to us, the controversial
Shroud of Turin) in turn spawned an endless number
of copies, more and more distant in appearance from
their model as time went on (the Russian Mandylions
bear little resemblance, other than the basic design, to
the first known Byzantine copies of the lost Edessan
original), but each as it were rendered authentic by
the chain of transmission from the primary image. The
same logic held true for the copies of the Images of the
Virgin and Child painted by Saint Luke, whose claim
to truth derived from the legend that they had been
painted in front of the models themselves. Presumably,
it was the apostle's Greek origins that qualified him as
the father of Christian painting; the obvious rationalist
critique, that never having met Christ in person, he
would have been hard-pressed to have painted him as
a baby in his mother's arms, had no impact whatsoever on the dissemination from the sixth century onward of the legend and the images it justified: what
mattered was that if such images of the Mother and
Child were to exist at all – and exist they had to, as the
cult of Mary flourished in Byzantium – they needed, if
they could not have appeared on their own as had the
Acheiropoieta, to have been painted from life, by an
eyewitness who through his talent (and with the help

of God) could guarantee the truth of the Image he had made.

The adoption of images by Christianity, however, also brought about a profound mutation in the manner of painting. The early Christian painters had inherited the techniques of Apelles and of the Fayyum portraits; yet, confronted with the task of expressing in images a radically different theological universe, they turned their backs on mimesis and subverted these techniques to create new forms, inventing what we still call the icon, a word that after all means nothing more, in Greek (*eikōn*), than 'image'. They began to introduce specific distortions of the human form, to cease to relate highlighting in the flesh tints to the illusion of an external light source, to eliminate highlighting altogether in the eyes, to surround the heads with elaborate halos that deeply modified their relation to the background, to develop an exciting and original treatment of colour, especially for the clothes and the space surrounding the figure, and to completely alter the perspectival organization of the pictorial space, flattening it and relating it to the viewer in a profoundly new way. This break with a realism so painfully acquired over centuries was deliberate, it derived, as Belting notes, from the will 'to free oneself from the limits of the physical world', to spiritualize the representation of bodies. Jean-Luc Godard, in his film *Notre Musique*, referring to a famous Byzantine icon recognized by Bernadette of Lourdes as the image of the woman she had seen in the grotto, sums up in a few words the essence of this art: 'No movement; no depth; no illusion whatsoever: the sacred.' As an Orthodox acquaintance explains to me, the figures in icons appear the way they do because they have already passed through death: 'The icons show not our world but the world after the Parousia, the world after the eighth day, the world to come.' If they are built upon what is called an 'inverse perspective', it is because the vanishing point is not the horizon, as in realist perspective, but the viewer's heart; it is not the viewer who is looking into the icon, but the icon that is looking out at the viewer.

An essay on Francis Bacon (who would certainly have appreciated what a friend writes to me in relation to the Iconoclastic Controversy: 'Think of how much blood there is in history, real blood, every time people decide to destroy images') is sadly no place to delve into the elaboration of a Christian theology of images; nor into the causes of the split between the Latin and the Greek tradition of images, which led to the development of what we have come to call art. The results of this protracted process fill our museums, and some of our churches: both in the East, where Russian Orthodoxy never departed from the Byzantine tradition, but continued to deepen it by seeking ever more spiritual depth through the distortion of the figure and the capacity of such distortions to convey pathos (reaching, with Theophanes the Greek and Andrei Rublyov, heights Byzantine painting never had); and in the West, where in thirteenth-century Italy painting abruptly and decisively broke with its theological framework, inventing, in little over a century, its own autonomous space, linked still to religious practices and values, but no longer defined in its forms by doctrinal imperatives. By the early fifteenth century a painter such as Rogier van der Weyden would be depicting himself as Saint Luke painting the Virgin and Child; and by 1521, as Hans Belting has shown, the modification of Lucas Cranach's signature, between his second and third portrait of Luther, from *cera lucae* ('the wax of Lucas') to *lucae opus* ('the work of Lucas'), has definitively sealed the revolution in practices. In *lucae opus*, of course, the men of those times immediately read the reference to the portraits made by Saint Luke, to the beginning of the history of Christian images; but these words also expressed the artist's bold new claim: 'In the jarring use of the word *opus*,' writes Belting, 'the image becomes a work of art and declares its aesthetical ambition.'

—

XXI

Everything would change, once again, with the eruption of photography. From the moment of its birth, photography staked out its claim to the production of true images, a claim later taken up by the cinema, and most outrageously stated (even if it was only, as he now says, 'a sentence made for talking, for thinking') by Jean-Luc Godard, in his second film *Le Petit Soldat*: 'Photography is truth, and cinema is twenty-four times truth per second.' The apparent validity of this exorbitant claim derived from photography's annexation of mimesis; no one at the time, certainly, was aware of its even deeper grounding in the earliest Christian notions of truth in images: photography was true because its images were not made by hands, and because they directly bore witness to the reality of what they represented, being both a trace of the thing itself and a proof of its existence at the moment the image was made. Bacon, like so many painters before him, fully recognized the implications of these facts: 'You know,' he once said to Franck Maubert, 'ever since its invention, photography has completely transformed painting and the vision of painters. Photography engenders other images.' Painting thus had little recourse but to drastically rethink itself, to drastically rethink the nature of its truth. And like the earliest icon painters, the inaugural gesture of the modernists – of Manet, closely followed by the impressionists and by Cézanne – was to break with mimesis, with imitation in painting, no longer, however, in the name of transcendence but in the name of the real. Photography, the painters ruefully acknowledged, could not be defeated on its own ground; even at its earliest, rudimentary stages, its claim to the faithful reproduction of reality could not be challenged. Painting would have to modify the terms of the debate, to change the very rules of the game, if it was to endure as a valid art form. Its survival, and the nagging sense of inferiority that still haunts photographers (those who bother to think about their medium, at least), is testimony to its success in doing so.

The parallel between modern and Byzantine painting is not new; as far as I know, it was first put forth in 1958 by the American critic Clement Greenberg, in a seminal essay entitled 'Byzantine Parallels'. The painters themselves had made it decades before; after the rediscovery of icon painting in the late nineteenth century, the first abstract painters directly compared their work to icons, especially Malevich, who went so far as to hang some of his pictures in the 'icon's corner' of his home. And it is no accident if the Renaissance painter who today appears the most 'modern' to us, El Greco, had begun his career, in Crete, as a painter of icons: 'the Greek manner teaches us fruitful difficulties,' he later wrote in the margins of his copy of Vasari's *Vite*. Rejecting, as El Greco did to a certain extent, the sculptural and perspectival nature of the Greco-Roman and the European tradition, modern painting would inaugurate the trend toward a *shallow space*, a 'progressive elimination of the representational', as

Greenberg puts it, brought about by the 'confinement to flat pictorial space'. For the art historian Michael Fried, the modernity of Manet's painting is due to the fact that the painting now faces the spectator, becomes a surface that gazes out at the spectator; the same quality, as we know, that Byzantine theologians sought in their icons. But the flattening of painting is not without risk: as in Byzantine art, where according to Greenberg 'light and shade were stylized into flat patterns and used for decorative or quasi-abstract ends instead of illusionist ones', the move towards shallow space threatened to blur 'the distinction between the decorative and the non-decorative'. *Decorative*, as we know, is a derogatory epithet frequently applied to certain forms of painting, not least by Bacon, who relished in dismissing abstract art as 'even at its very best . . . never more than local, charming and decorative.' Yet one could also consider the decorative in art not as a quality (or a deficiency) in itself but as the extreme end of a spectrum, the other end of which would be illusion in depth; and it is indeed from the tension generated by the simultaneous rejection of both extremes that modern painting draws its greatest strengths. This holds true for figurative as well as abstract painters. If Rothko's painting is so powerful, it is precisely because it is resolutely not decorative, because it not only flattens the pictorial space but simultaneously resists this flatness, not however through an illusion of depth but through the creation of presence, a presence that quietly hovers just in front of or behind the ground, thickening it or hollowing it out, bringing it alive. This is the difference between shallow space and flat space, probably the key to all that is best in abstract painting, from Malevich and Kandinsky to Rothko. The charge of decorativeness has of course often been leveled against Bacon himself. American critics especially, even today, still persist in opposing his work to that of the abstract expressionists, as if the achievements of the latter somehow disqualified the former. As recently as the latest retrospective the critic of *The New Yorker* (and he was far from alone) could write, in all good faith, that 'in the mid-century contest for a radically new and befitting Western art, my countrymen [Rothko and Pollock] played fair, and Bacon cheated.' I tend to suspect that the reiteration of such charges, over decades, has as much to do with American criticism's visceral Puritanism as with its instinctive suspicion of all things European: Bacon, after all, is the first artist to have painted nude males, and quite beautifully at that, in the act of defecating or being penetrated; whereas abstract art, of course, shows no bodies at all. Be that as it may, I would on the contrary suggest – the idea would certainly have appaled the painters concerned – that in their fundamentals Bacon's and Rothko's art are not so far apart. As Gilles Deleuze points out in his study *Bacon: The Logic of Sensation*, there are only two ways of escaping mimesis: 'by extraction or by isolation', that is towards abstraction or towards what he calls 'the figural'; different means, but to a similar purpose. And seen through the prism of Byzantine painting, even the means are not so wildly different. Bacon would certainly not have taken issue with some of the statements issued by Rothko, together with his friend Adolph Gottlieb, in a June 1943 letter to the critic Edward Alden Jewell: 'We favor the simple expression of the complex thought. We are for the large shape because it has the impact of the unequivocal. We wish to reassert the picture plane. We are for flat forms because they destroy illusion and reveal truth.' Both Bacon and Rothko considered their paintings as in a sense a 'theatre' or an 'arena'; both reasoned in terms of shallow space; and both understood, and mastered, the use of tonal as opposed to value contrast to manipulate this space as well as to convey primal emotions. Even when they came to different, sometimes even antithetical solutions, they were most often addressing the same problem, for instance the painting's relation to the wall, which both considered a key issue: Rothko, notoriously, insisted that his pictures not be framed at all, and painted their edges, aiming to open a space in the wall and thus in his words 'to make the rooms more rooms'; Bacon on the contrary had his set in heavy gilded frames and covered in glass, a device that not only serves, as many critics have pointed out, to unify the field but also to cut off the painted space from the wall, restoring depth in and of itself, no matter how shallow the space of the image. Remains the

figure: Rothko first made it symbolic and then aban-
doned it altogether, whereas Bacon, on the contrary,
ever more decisively made it the core of his work. But
Rothko always insisted that his art was not in fact 'abstract', that it was 'realistic', as he told William Seitz in
January 1952, three years after achieving his so-called
mature style; 'it was not,' Seitz recorded in his notes,
'that the figures had been *removed* . . . but that the
symbols for the figures, and in turn the shapes in the
later canvases were new *substitutes* for the figures. . . .
My new areas of colour [says Rothko] are things. I put
them on the surface. They do not run to the edge, they
stop before the edge.' Since then, the American scholar
Anne Chase has led the way in showing how Rothko's
'abstract' paintings continue to draw on the long-
established codes of figurative painting to present a
new type of figure, a 'subject in abstraction'. Daniel
Arasse has taken the idea even further: for him, the
progressive erasure of the figure in Rothko's work, its
disappearance, 'would be as its Assumption', in the
sense in which the Virgin in her Assumption leaves behind her tomb, 'the present figure of her absence'. We
know the significance that the Shoah, as well as the
earlier tsarist pogroms, had for Rothko, a Jewish im-
migrant from present-day Latvia; he persistently re-
ferred to the importance of 'intimations of mortality'
for his painting, instinctively grasping the fundamental
relationship between images and death. It is this prox-
imity with death that brings Bacon the closest to

Rothko. 'You may say we're always attempting to defeat death by leaving images,' Bacon told Melvyn Bragg in 1985, 'but it won't make any difference.' The knowledge didn't stop him from striving, with the same single-minded determination as Rothko, and using means equally artificial, to achieve an image that would incarnate the sensation of living of a being that knows that it is faced with death. In a way, to our modern sensibility, the true image is always an image of death; we see this clearly in photography, one of the first uses of which was to provide families with images of the deceased, and where the ultimate image, the ultimate icon, is always the picture of the instant of death, of death *as it is happening* (Robert Capa in Spain, Eddie Adams in Saigon, the Zapruder film; Leonardo Henrichsen, in Chile, filming his own death). In his *Histoire(s) du Cinéma*, Godard, citing Blanchot, mournfully intones in his slow deep voice: 'Yes, the image is bliss – but close by dwells nothingness, and the image can only express its full power by calling upon it.' And he continues, as does Blanchot: 'The image, capable of negating nothingness, is also the gaze of nothingness upon us.'

—

F17: 163

Z FRAME 313: The fatal impact. The President's head is obscured in a grotesque halo of blood and brains as a bullet slams into the right side of his skull. The bullet's explosive impact sends blood, brains, and skull fragments forward as well as down and rearward.

For Bacon, the question of the 'true image' was a question of realism. His friend Michel Leiris placed this problem at the heart of the last and finest essay he devoted to him, *Face and Profile*, published in 1983. Quoting a letter Bacon had sent him, in which the painter, writing in French, defined realism as 'the attempt to capture appearance with all the sensations which that particular appearance awake in me', Leiris sought to apprehend it as 'a creative realism . . . and not only a transcribing one, a realism that tends less to figure a reality than to institute it.' In the same letter, Bacon had written: 'Perhaps realism, in its most profound expression, is always subjective.' This was a long-held belief, one he had already expressed nearly two decades earlier to David Sylvester: 'When you paint anything, you are at the same time also painting not only the subject but you are painting yourself as well. . . . Because painting is a dual performance. If I look at a Rembrandt painting, I feel I know much more about Rembrandt than I do about the sitter.' This appeal to subjectivity, as opposed to the cold objectivity of photography, as an essential component of any new, any modern realism in painting, strikes me as very Albertinian, but paradoxically so; for Alberti, it was imitation in painting, and the invention of perspective, that were to be associated with the myth of Narcissus: 'What is painting but the act of embracing, by means of art, the surface of the pool?' he famously wrote in 1435 (the same year van der Weyden painted his self-portrait as Saint Luke), in a text that names Narcissus as the inventor of painting. I'll leave aside here the question of the narcissistic structure of Bacon's painting in order to consider the manner in which, in his struggle against 'illustration' in art, he associates artifice with the subjectivity he placed at the core of his realism. Bacon always insisted that his art was inherently artificial, that, in the words of his biographer Michael Peppiatt, 'artifice reveals truth'. Talking once again with David Sylvester, sometime in the early 1980s, Bacon commented:

In one of his letters Van Gogh speaks of the need to make changes in reality, which become lies that are truer than the literal truth. This is the only possible way the painter can bring back the intensity of the reality which he is trying to capture. I believe that reality in art is something profoundly artificial and that it has to be recreated.

While Peppiatt associates Bacon's love of artifice in painting with his sexual tastes, in particular his lifelong passion for female underwear and makeup, I would suggest that it has as much to do with his obsession with photography. Though he ostensibly relegated it to the limbo of 'illustration', it is obvious that Bacon took photography, and the challenge it posed to painting and to the making of images in general, deadly seriously. He was certainly fascinated by photographs. The retrospective at the Metropolitan, like at the Prado (and at the Tate, where I didn't see it), displayed some of the countless pictures that he kept stacked in deep piles in his studio, stepped on, doodled on, paint-stained, crushed, torn, mishandled. A recent book by Martin Harrison entitled *Incunabula* offers a broad selection and shows in some detail the manifold ways in which the painter manipulated the images he found or had made, such as for instance folding them in a highly calculated manner, and then pinning or clipping them, to obtain distortions of the figure he could then exploit in painting. As the book demonstrates, Bacon would cull his source material from just about anywhere, glossy magazines, art books, film stills, scientific and medical works, technical manuals, wildlife albums, sports papers, bodybuilding booklets, gay pornography, postcards, street scenes. 'Remember that I look at everything,' he often repeated. Yet even though this collection supplied him with as vast a sampling as possible of the relentless production of images of his century, there was nothing random in the selection. Bacon's eye for the significant detail, the detail that he could strip from its context and make use of, was incredibly acute: ripped from a magazine and tossed into one of his crates, a banal news photograph of Marilyn Monroe sitting in a white dress is suddenly revealed as a very Baconian flow of flesh ('I've always liked the positioning of it very much,' he told an interviewer he showed this image to). Unlike the surrealists and a number of his contemporaries, however, he never made direct use of photographs in his painting, by collaging them or copying them as such, with the exception of the portraits he reproduced as pinned photographs in his 1973 *Three Portraits* or in his last great narcissian *Triptych*, painted in 1991. For him, photographs were working material, fertilizer for ideas, a vast dictionary of forms, no more. It is all the more curious, then, that whereas Bacon never painted himself paintbrush in hand, he did twice depict himself wielding a camera, making an image mechanically, an 'illustration': in his 1970 *Triptych – Studies from the Human Body*, and a few years later in a *Triptych – March 1974*, in which the figure of the painter, his face hidden behind a camera, copied from an actual Polaroid self-portrait taken in a mirror, steps out from behind a large canvas with its back turned to the viewer – the lower corner, perhaps, of the canvas Velázquez depicted himself painting in *Las Meninas*?

Deleuze, in his book on Bacon, states that in spite of his fascination, 'he recognizes no aesthetic value in photographs. . . . In spite of all his surrender [to them], Bacon has a radical hostility to photography.' I would agree with Deleuze that a powerful ambiguity lies at the heart of Bacon's complex relation to photography, and by extension to film. It seems as if for him, in the end, and in spite of all his dismissals, photography was the only serious challenger, perhaps because its monopolistic claim to the production of true images is, to a certain extent, so deeply grounded in the Western artistic tradition, and to a broader extent in the human relation to images. This ambiguous relationship, then, might

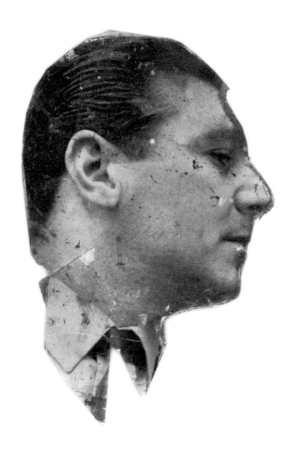

serve to illuminate some of Bacon's most essential artistic choices. For if photography's truth, like those of the Images of Saint Luke, derives to a large extent from the fact that it forms not just an image but also a trace, and thus a proof of the real presence of its subject at the moment it was made, Bacon, by contrast, will resolutely refuse to paint from life, accepting only to work from reproductions (true or not, the story of how he failed, while living in Rome for several months, to go and see the original of Velázquez's *Portrait of Pope Innocent X* he had so often copied has formed part of his legend), or from photographs of his models, photographs he began in the 1960s to have specially made to order for him by his friend John Deakin, according to precise instructions. And if the other basis of photography's authority is the mechanical origin of the images it produces, images, like the Acheiropoieta, 'not made by human hands', then Bacon will insist on the importance of the painter's hand in his work, on the importance of the traces made, unmade, remade, and finally left behind by that unreliable hand. John Richardson, a British art historian who knew Bacon well, has recently given us in the *New York Review of Books* a remarkably hilarious description of the manner in which the self-taught painter would practice his technique:

On an early visit to the studio, I watched Francis experiment. Ensconced in front of a mirror, he rehearsed on his own face the brushstrokes that he envisaged making on canvas. With a flourish of his wrist, he would apply great swoops of Max Factor 'pancake' makeup in a gamut of flesh colors to the stubble on his chin. The makeup adhered to the stubble much as the paint would adhere to the unprimed verso of the canvas that he used in preference to the smooth, white-primed recto.

Peter Beard, whom Bacon often painted in the 1970s and who on occasion watched him work, described the physicality of Bacon's gestures to an interviewer: 'He obviously did weird things, like accidentally rub against the thing, or his shoulder [sic], or blowing dust, or – Roaaar! [waving his arms about] – trying to get a thing that doesn't work completely different.' Bacon would go to lengths to underline the gestures made by his hands, flinging white balls of paint at his pictures or adding arrows to point to a felicitous detail. At the Met, coming once again upon his vibrant and elegiac 1949 *Study from the Human Body*, I noticed for the first time how the two little white arrows painted on the figure's shoulders point straight at a bold white vertebra protruding from its neck, a resolutely unnatural and artificial vertebra, derived from Bacon's reading of the backs of some of Degas' pastel female nudes, and used here with remarkable effect to intensify the whole reality of the neck and shoulders and of the sad tilt of the head: 'Look,' the arrows say to the spectator, 'this is how I was made, this is what makes this image true, what 'flips it back onto your nervous system.' Further along in the show hangs his 1962 *Three Studies for a*

Crucifixion, a breakthrough painting for him, which he casually admitted having created in the course of a two-week-long drinking binge. The man writhing on the mattress, in the center panel, is perhaps one of Bacon's most phenomenal passages of pure painting; every time I see it, the paint simply mesmerizes me, the bold swoops, swirls, jabs, dips, cross-strokes, downward smears, with the pigment appearing to flow freely in the medium, a form of 'action painting' perhaps, but that coheres to produce a figure, a great figure. When Bacon finally came out of his alcoholic frenzy, he found tiny dabs of paint spattered all over the canvas; and when he then filled in the background, painting in the black blinds, he didn't recover these bits but left them circled, quite visible, telling us that what is important in this painting, what makes it real, is how it was made. And even in his relatively more disciplined productions, Bacon seemed to know that more than a matter of the painter's eye painting is a matter of the painter's hand, and that as the hand is often faster than the eye, the eye can only follow, record, analyze, and perhaps modify the marks already made, a far cry from the *cosa mentale* of a Leonardo or a Velázquez.

Numerous critics and painters have commented on Bacon's technical limitations. Damien Hirst claims that Bacon's feet are 'bloody awful', a rather bold generalization if one is to consider the lovely poised foot of the right-hand figure in the 1970 *Triptych – Studies of the Human Body* or the dramatically projected foot, grasping a key, of the 1978 *Painting*, which show, at the very least, that if Bacon often painted his figures' lower limbs like club feet, it was because he wanted to. John Richardson has made a more compelling case about Bacon's lack of draftsmanship, a limitation Bacon was keenly aware of and willingly confessed to ('I can't draw,' he told BBC radio in one of his last recorded interviews. 'If you asked me to draw something I don't think I'd be able to.') But for me such remarks, which follow Malraux's view that 'we only, without remorse, dare call masterpieces those works that allow us to believe, as secretly as it may be, in the mastery of man', are besides the point. Like Rothko, who long struggled to paint convincing figures, like all great artists, Bacon succeeded precisely by turning his technical limitations into his strengths. It works the same way in literature: Nabokov might well have been the greatest lyrical prose stylist, in English, of the twentieth century, yet his writing remains fundamentally hollow, because he devotes all his considerable skill and his magical ear to the avoidance of his inner demons, to the weaving of shimmering fantasies that studiously elude the questions that truly mattered to him as a human being; whereas Faulkner, whose prose, though it can on occasion rise to a mesmerizing pitch, all too often comes out labored or awkward, somehow wrestled his imperfect tool into a thing so imperious it could drive the reader's face into a swamp and hold it there until he is on the verge of suffocation, only allowing him the briefest of gasps before plunging him back in, and leaving him, at the end, with hardly even the strength to weep. Deleuze clearly states Bacon's essential idea: 'In art . . . the question is not to reproduce or to invent forms, but to capture forces.' And to capture the forces he sought, Bacon came up with numerous inventions: his spaces, for instance, the oddly structured spaces his figures evolve in, trapped together with the spectator in a claustrophobic face-to-face whose pressure, at its highest point of intensity, crushes the one onto the other. Much has already been written about these spaces, and I will not repeat it here, but I would like to note, in relation to what I ventured earlier about Byzantine painting, their shallow quality. The flat, strongly coloured backgrounds, often painted in acrylics or household emulsions, that offset the figure are far from the only method Bacon deployed to achieve this shallowness. There is of course a form of perspective in Bacon's spaces, an odd distorted perspective that nonetheless does give a sense of depth to the works; these paintings are never 'as thick as a playing card', as critics held Manet's to be (Courbet once famously compared *Olympia* to 'the Queen of Hearts after a bath'). Yet while he leaves these spaces open, letting some air and light circulate through them, he simultaneously brings into play an array of methods to flatten them. Consider what he does in his 1974 *Sleeping Figure*, a nude self-portrait set in a room on a plain bed. One of the most obvious features of the painting is a black oval painted around the figure's penis, an oval that for many will evoke the halo Christian painters placed around the heads of their Christs and their saints. But to read this as a metaphorical device ironically sanctifying the figure's sex would probably be an error. Bacon, like all painters, knew that a halo, well before its symbolic function comes into play, is first and foremost a visual device, one that (especially in its pre-Renaissance versions) pulls the figure's head off the picture plane and deliberately separates it from the background. Here, it's the contrary: the see-through halo is placed not only in front of the figure but in front of the door frame that serves to define the exterior of the glass room the figure inhabits. It also has exactly the same shape and size as the brown oval halo surrounding the light bulb hung over the figure, a brown which, as one of the few warm colours in the composition, quite naturally draws the halo toward the viewer: the overall effect is that the two halos, between them, compress the picture space, the one around the light bulb drawing the room out while the other one forcefully drives the framing door in onto the figure, causing (together with the way the beige floor is depicted and the use of a cold purple blob to the lower left that pushes that angle back) the entire room to tilt, up and toward us, tipping the figure off the bed, pinned as it were between it and the glass door. A similar effect can be observed in the 1976 *Figure in Movement*, where the black circle around the head, set against the hot orange of the floor (and designated to our attention by an arrow) pulls it toward us at the same time as the black circle set above the figure's buttocks, doubling them, shoves them backward, violently compressing the body in relation to the framing device, twisting it into the painfully erotic position before us.

The play between hot and cold colours to obtain spatial effects is a constant of Bacon's mature style, and it is what makes him a true colourist. Deleuze, for instance, has commented at length on the variations of gray and orange that mold the flesh of the figures of the 1970 *Three Studies of the Male Back*. In a slightly earlier painting, the 1969 *Lying Figure*, the figure appears to be neither lying nor even falling backward; on the contrary, the warm yellow-gold halo around the light bulb, trapped between the very pale purple background and a rising sheet of the same colour, literally sucks the figure upward, knees first, out of the dirty muddy greens and the cold blues and blacks of the lower half of the canvas. One could go on. In the small portraits of the 1960s and 1970s, some of Bacon's finest works, the even featureless backgrounds behind the heads, painted in a variety of colours, alternatively bright or dull, in oil or in synthetic paint, again function like the gold halo that fills the painting frame of so many Byzantine icons: the painting is flattened, it fully faces you and looks out at you, the same way an icon or a Rothko looks out at you, the head comes straight off this flatness yet is part of this 'facingness', as Michael Fried calls it, the head is there,

XXIV

as real as any real head. In a lovely 1969 *Self-Portrait*, to take but one example, the face is set off from the (very cold) teal background by delicate, warm orange and pink lines; as for the shirt or jacket, it is depicted as flat, with no depth, yet the collar, brown tinged with dark green, comes forward off the teal as well as the blue T-shirt under it because it is a much warmer colour, while the shoulders, warm too, but made of raw canvas left unpainted, also rise from the teal while drawing back from the collar; the whole garment thus subtly taking on depth to define, together with the brown cowlick at the top (brown paint on raw canvas left showing), a shallow space in which the head, painted with a blend of hot and cold colours (including touches of the teal) that either slash through or are tamped down above muddy colours applied in broad, fast, thick swirling strokes, suddenly *comes together*. It is completed with a precise round white dab on the chin and a long thin white stroke running down the nose, the same white stroke added as a final highlight in so many of the Fayyum portraits, yet used here not for its value, as light, but for its tone, as colour, and thus placed at the service of an entirely different intent, the making of a radically different sort of true image.

As Deleuze notes, there is a very strong tendency in Bacon's paintings toward the fall. Things fall, collapse, and even more often flow down: in some images, it is as if the flesh were melting off the bones. Often, it flows into a strange blob that is not quite a shadow: a 'flesh shadow', Bacon called it in his notes, a blob of colour, made of nothing more than paint itself, functioning as the pool of paint into which this painted Narcissus is slowly dissolving, 'his life flowing out of him' (as the painter once said of the Dyer figure in his *Triptych – August 1972*), unless, in yet another variation, the figure grows out of the pool, flower and flesh in one, a reverse Narcissus. And when the blob does darken and stretch out and begin to resemble a shadow more, it is the shadow of death, like the one flowing out of the central Dyer figure in the *Triptych – May-June 1973*, the dying Dyer, his shadow shaped like an Erinyes. 'Make shadow into separate unit,' Bacon once scrawled on a leaf, torn out of an edition of Muybridge, showing a beautiful male nude swinging his fist. Yet he firmly rejected the symbolic interpretation, ventured for instance by Michael Peppiatt, that his shadows served 'as a constant reminder of death – the ever-lengthening darkness that 'shadows' every life': 'They have nothing to do with mortality,' he affirmed in his last BBC interview. 'They have to do with the layout of the painting, that's all.' For once, it might be worth taking him at his word. In the left-hand panel of the first great triptych he painted after Dyer's death, the 1971 *Triptych – In Memory of George Dyer*, the shadow of the stricken Dyer-boxer figure is, unusually, rather realistically depicted. Yet there is no 'ground' for it to be projected on; it behaves rather as something expelled from the figure, a wonderfully artificial device, a shadow of

paint, cast onto paint. Bacon, naturally, knew of Giotto's refusal to paint cast shadows: for how could an
image, any more than the souls in Dante's Purgatorio,
cast a shadow? It would not be until Masaccio, and
the full blooming of scientific perspective and sculptural imitation in painting, that the first cast shadows
(those of Adam and Eve expelled from Eden) would
appear on a canvas. Shadows, 'the sign of true bodies' as Hans Belting writes, of course saturate the pho-
tographic space: as much as with light, photographs
are made with shadows, to such an extent that William Fox Talbot, one of the pioneers of photography,
hesitated between this name and that of skiagraphy,
'shadow painting'. But with Bacon we are talking of
something completely different: this is not the shadow
left by a true body blocking a source of light, it is the
shadow, made of paint, spilled by a body made of paint
onto a painted ground. It's the painter's shadow that
Bacon once dreamed of, as he recounted it to Peppiatt:
'I was going down a street and my shadow was going
along the wall with me, and I thought, Ah, perhaps
this might help me with my painting, and I reached
out and tore the shadow off.' What we see in the painting, then, is the shadow when it is removed from the
world of light and of bodies, and is carried over into
the world of paint. It is the same with the pale yellow-
purple blob flowing out of the stricken boxer's arm: if
the life is to flow out of him, it will flow not in blood
or in the form of an immaterial soul, it will flow out in

paint. And it is the same with the murder weapon, the cricket ball Bacon rendered with such a velvety perfection: if you look closely, the shadow it seems to cast on the yellowish blob (in a direction opposite from the boxer's shadow) is no shadow at all, it is dark red, the ball is coated in blood, after smashing into the boxer's face it has bounced down onto the canvas, onto the painted blob, rolling and leaving behind a neat red smear of painted blood. If Bacon's paintings are true images, it is first and foremost because they are true, in every detail of their composition, to their nature as painted images, as images made in paint.

XXV

— List of Plates —

— Author's Note —

I would like to express my gratitude to a number of people whose help and friendship contributed to the preparation of this book.

First and foremost, Manuela Mena Marqués, who opened the doors of the Prado for me, and with whom the dialogue on painting and art has not ceased since.

James Atlas, who insisted that a diptych become a triptych.

At the Dublin City Gallery The Hugh Lane, Jessica O'Donnell, as well as her director Barbara Dawson and her colleagues Margarita Cappock and Elisabeth Forster, who gave me unrestricted access to their collections and to their archive of Francis Bacon's studio documents.

José Capelo, for his generous gesture, as well as Luc Delahaye.

Pierre Monestier.

For their advice or their research: Jannic Durand, chief curator of the Department of Decorative Arts of the Louvre; Emilia Philippot, curator at the Réunion des musées nationaux; Philippe Comar, professor at the École des beaux-arts; Francisco Rico, professor at the Autonomous University of Barcelona; and Philippe Demanet.

Julia Ede at Andrew Nurnberg Associates.

Though these three essays were written in English, the first edition of the book was the French one, published by L'Arbalète Gallimard. It was designed in collaboration with Thomas Simonnet, whom I thank again for his enthusiasm, his creativeness, his support, and his patience throughout the editorial process.

J.L.

nh